Sister Vero

The Echoes of Priest

by

Fr. Tom Grufferty

Inspiring and Practical Pastoral experiences for every Christian

With

Blessings Galore.

Tom Grufferty

Book Dedication

These Echoes are nearly all about people especially those people who enriched my life and my ministry. I would like to dedicate this book to them in great love and a in thanksgiving for the enormous contribution they have made to me personally.

"Rivers do not drink their own water.

trees do not eat their own fruit.

the sun does not shine on itself and flowers do not

spread their fragrance for themselves.

Living for others is a rule of nature. We are born to

help each other.

No matter how difficult it is.

Life is good when you are happy but much better when

others are happy because of you.

Let us remember that pain is a sign that we are alive,

problems are a sign that we are strong, and prayer is a

sign that we are not alone.

If we can acknowledge these truths and condition our

hearts and minds, our lives will be more meaningful,

different and worthwhile."

(POPE FRANCIS)

Foreword

By Bishop Crispian Hollis

Foreword for "The Echoes of a Parish Priest"

It is a brave parish priest who puts his thoughts and reflections into the hands of his former bishop for commendation and – perhaps – comment, but Fr Tom need have no fear. It has been a pleasure for me to have been able to revisit the ministry I have shared with him over 23 years in the diocese of Portsmouth (1989 -2012). I have always admired his work for the Lord, though he may not have always been aware of that. Over the years, through varying degrees of closeness, we have developed a solid friendship and, I think, great mutual respect.

These pages provide a fascinating and impressive record of the immense variety that marks and illustrates the life of a pastoral priest in the life of a busy and varied diocese. You must read on through this story for the details of that and I am not going to be the one who provides a "spoiler alert" for you, the reader.

My first encounter with Tom was when I was a very new bishop on visitation, and he was parish priest in Basingstoke. He worked me hard on that weekend and I ended up preaching and/or celebrating 9 Masses, on the basis that the people wanted to meet their new bishop. I got home very tired that evening!

This experience was not the reason for Tom's subsequent move to St Joseph's in Havant, but it was there that I began to get to know him and appreciate those rich and varied qualities and experiences which have made him the excellent priest that he is, and which are extensively offered to us in these pages.

This little volume makes a fascinating read and it

shows us many of the individual gifts and enthusiasms which remain undiminished in Tom, even though he is now officially in retirement. But then, as I have discovered for myself, priests don't really retire; they simply allow a new chapter to be opened up in their lives as disciples. New opportunities, a deeper sense of prayer and commitment, new challenges, failures, and successes - ministry and service remain the hallmarks of what is involved in being a priest in our Catholic communities. Retirement from active ministry removes us from office, but, by no means, from service and commitment.

Service is always the key, and never privilege or honour, and the example of the Lord is always before us. "I have given you", says Jesus, "an example so that you may copy what I have done for you…you must love one another, just as I have loved you. It is by your love for one another that everyone will recognise you as my disciples."

These pages are truly the story of one who is a faithful disciple of the Lord.

+Crispian Hollis

Introduction

As a young man growing up in the West of Ireland, I was fortunate enough to be raised in a family who loved both the written and spoken word. Looking back to that time in my life, I feel sure that my love of literature and the arts originated from those days living with my parents. They nurtured in us, not only the importance of a good education, but how one can appreciate the beauty of the world around us, by really seeing what we were looking at and reading about.

So, on the Grufferty bookshelves I recall the much-read works of Joyce, Shakespeare of course and many art books containing the wonderful paintings which are still confirmed as masterpieces to this day.

I am sure that if I delved into the several boxes containing my life's possessions, I would find a couple of the books from those days. The leather covers much worn now, of course, but I am sure, illustrating how much those pages were cherished, due to the number of times they had been read by me and my four brothers and one sister.

This combination of words and images is one reason why I have written this book which I have called *Echoes*. I have carefully chosen *"Echoes"* because I wanted to share with you, the real-life events, the images, the highs, and lows of parish life which reverberate in me to this day. These various elements have formed me into the person I have become. I can assure you that I am in a vastly different place now than when I was ordained in 1973. As you read the following pages, you will note that I have designed the chapters so that you follow Church events based on the Liturgical Year as a journey of faith.

When I finally left home to join the great Irish migration to the U.K., I know my parents felt that they had given me as good a start in life as they could, and the rest was now up to me. What did I take with me? Well the first thing would be a love of words, how engaging they are, what colours one can paint with them figuratively speaking and, I suppose, how powerful they can be.

During my training for the priesthood at All Hallows College in Dublin, we were taught how to become philosophers and theologians, even footballers. All sound advice and guidance. However, what was missing for me, was the importance of words. Such a key part of homilies, discussions, and chats is the use of words. As any priest will tell you, one spends a great deal of energy and time, selecting the right words for all events in the life of the Church, from Baptisms, to Weddings and Funerals and all that comes in between. Those words are remembered by all who hear them, so we aim to choose them well.

When I was planning this book, I thought about the evenings I would spend both as a seminarian and a young priest, listening to Alistair Cooke's "Letter from America" on the radio. What a storyteller he was, and so engaging, that there were occasions I wished his programme would never end. The images that he created were truly inspiring and demonstrated his clear love of the English language, which resonated with me.

Cooke also inspired me to travel, for the way he described world-events encouraged me to see for myself, other places and to meet other people from all walks of life. So it was that a young Grufferty, along with other seminarians, took up summer jobs in the U.S.A. enjoying every moment and so very different from where I had been brought up. This broadened our horizons enormously and gave us pocket money for the rest of the academic year.

Over the years, I have met so many wonderful people, especially those in parishes in which I have worked, who have both inspired and taught me the inner meanings of life. Among these generous souls are writers, artists and fellow clergy. Not without humour I am glad to say. Their echoes, even from those who have died resonate with me daily. We clergy underestimate the huge contribution made by the laity of our parishes.

In this book, I have used the opportunity to indulge in my deep-rooted love of literature – selecting homilies from past times, poems, and articles that I have written for different occasions over the last 47 years.

Of course, as powerful as words are, so also are images. I find I use both more in the work that I produce and which you will discover as you explore my book. The Church has successfully used both for centuries. Renaissance art is so powerful that we do not need words at all, Caravaggio and Michelangelo interpret the Word of God so vividly. When I visit an Art Gallery, I often watch people reading about the painting they are looking at. You can see the revelatory moment on their face when they discover its meaning.

Echoes is a kaleidoscope of my life from describing the importance of words, images and magnificent art pieces, my life as a priest, my love of travel including the many pilgrimages which I have led and been a part of over the years. All these experiences have contributed enormously to my spiritual bank account. I invite you, dear reader, to enter the Holy Ground with enthusiasm, faith, and love.

Get in contact with your own "Echoes" so that you can discover new visions resounding in your personal journey as a believer

What follows are some of the more important things I have written about or pondered on for the last 47 years of priesthood. I have used the liturgical year as a framework of these Echoes.

Most of these reflections have been published in *The Tablet, The Furrow, The Pastoral Review, Intercom, Portsmouth People, Catholic South West*, with permission from all the Editors. I also acknowledge the outstanding co-operation and encouragement from these same people.

Father Tom Grufferty

The Liturgical Year

Advent –

Preparation to Welcome All for Christmas - Fling the Church Doors Open

Christmas is a glorious opportunity to pull out all the stops in offering hospitality to all those who cross the threshold of the church. This "Welcome Home" promotion can be done at any time. Every Catholic in the pew, and those outside, needs to know that they deserve a second chance, since we have a God of the second chance. It is amazing how mean we have been with forgiveness; but with the whole idea of forgiveness, we have placed a bounty on mercy. Even as we welcome people, we need to examine carefully what they will find when they come back. Every Sunday we celebrate a treasure of immeasurable proportions, but according to Pope Francis, we sometimes leave Mass as if we have been to a funeral.

We need to make sure that what we give returnees is much more than they received before they left us. It goes without saying that we need to probe why "out of touch Catholics" left us in the first place and make sure they do not find the same things which originally drove them out. Every parish needs to re- evaluate the following points. I consider these to be the 12 commandments of a warm, welcoming community: -

- *Keep an open church during the week.*
- *Begin the welcome in the church car park.*
- *Continue the welcome at the church door.*
- *Welcome everyone at the start of Mass.*
- *Offer a lively and uplifting liturgy.*
- *Enrich the celebration with music.*
- *Have a good sound system & visual aid.*

- ***Preach a meaningful, inspiring homily.***
- ***Ensure the church is warm and well lit.***
- ***Use the space in the church porch wisely.***
- ***Give care to all during and after Mass.***
- ***Genuinely invite people to come again.***

All children attending Mass should be acknowledged at the start of the Service even if they do not have their own Liturgy of the Word. They behave much better if their presence is acknowledged, and the following Sunday there will be more children at Mass. Children are the modern-day missionaries to each other and their families. Children should be involved in the Welcoming Ministry because they do it naturally. They just love giving out Hymn Books.

When Pope Francis compares the family to the parish, he clearly points out that children must be at the heart of the parish. For decades, they have been so, in our Catholic schools, but we need to make stronger bonds between what happens in the Catholic school and what happens at the Sunday Eucharist.

Young people too need to be engaged in ministry, especially as musicians, catechists, readers, and Extraordinary Ministers of Holy Communion. Having prepared the community, we are now ready for the real work. We are asking Catholics to be missionaries. They will never be good missionaries unless they learn how to welcome and how to offer mercy.

We need to walk in the shoes of those who have left the Church. The reasons why they have left are many and varied; some have been deeply hurt, and some are truly angry. If we can empathise with them, then we shall understand better the difficulties they may suffer when they attempt to return.

I have heard of people who made several attempts to come back, only to drive straight out of the car park.

That is one good reason why welcoming Catholics back, begins in the church car park. The Knights of St Columba perform wonderful acts of hospitality on special occasions in church car parks, but every Sunday Mass is a special occasion, and may be extra special for someone.

The next step a returnee must take is towards the entrance to the church building itself. If this is home, then it must be warm, inviting and a good place to be. Most church porches are full of clutter which serves no useful purpose whatsoever.

We really need to spend money on the entrances to our churches. As the Bishop's Chaplain to Head Teachers and Principals of all the Catholic Schools in Portsmouth Diocese, the contrast between the School porch and the Church porch could not be more marked. On entering the school, you immediately know the aims of this place of learning, but you would be hard pressed to find the Mission Statement in most of our Churches.

Many returnees must negotiate a new relationship with the Church and with the Lord. This will certainly not be easy for them and it may be uncomfortable for us too because we have taken so much for granted. It would be wrong for those who have never left the Church to think that the return of the exile presents no major challenges once they have made the move to return.

A newly recovered faith in the Lord leaves many floundering. A warm welcome is vital, but we need to walk alongside people. Accompany them during Mass because words and actions may have changed since they left. Invite them to refreshments after Mass, and make sure they are never left isolated. Listen carefully to what they have to say because they will have a lot of questions. As the people leave, make sure they are invited back; walk with them to the car park to let them know that this is a loving and caring community.

(Citation: GRUFFERTY, T. December 2015. *The Tablet*).

Advent – The Return of the King

In St. Joseph's, Havant we always had special Advent Services on Sunday afternoon. Below I describe how I introduced the idea in 2005.

I have been reflecting and praying about the return of the King in the person of Jesus Christ. The four weeks leading up to Christmas are about the three Advents of Christ Our King.

The first is the Advent of Christ the King in time – it occurred two thousand years ago, in Bethlehem. Even in the humble surroundings of Bethlehem, there were some signs that this child, born in a stable, was destined for great things. Mary is told 'He will be great and be called son of the highest. God will give Him the throne of His ancestor David; He will rule over the house of Jacob forever and His reign will have no end' (Luke 1:32-34). Notice all the references to the King. The shepherds came to worship and the wise men from the east brought their special gifts. It is significant that one of those gifts was for royalty.

The second great coming of the King of Kings is in the daily lives of the faith community. He comes in the Eucharist in the form of Word, Bread and Wine. This presence is even more profound than the first. It is equally mysterious and wonderfully magnificent. The King of Kings is appearing at a church near you this Christmas. You are invited this Christmas to worship with the shepherds. Come to the manger, which is a throne.

Bring your royal gifts for your King. Masses at Christmas Midnight and on Christmas Day itself will make present once more the King of Kings, the Lord of Lords. He comes in the Mass to feed and strengthen His people, to forgive our sins and to sustain us on the journey of life. You are welcome to Church even if you have not been in touch for some time, in fact people like you are especially welcome!

The third coming of the Lord is The Return of the King at the end of time. As in the dream world of Tolkien, so in the real world of eternity, there will be freedom and peace for all the people. Tolkien wrote out of fiction and fantasy; the coming of the Kingdom of God is for real. We are members of the Kingdom of truth and love. Like the exotic world of Tolkien, we too need a strong king who will fight the forces of evil with us. Our power is neither in a ring nor in any other thing in Middle Earth, but in the one who came in history, comes in our time, and will come when He draws all things into completion. Christ our King wants to redeem everybody and everything.

I wish you a happy and holy Christmas and may The Return of the King bring you blessings in abundance.

(Citation: GRUFFERTY, T. December 2015. Homily)

Gaudete Sunday - the Third Sunday of Advent

'Gaudete' is Latin for rejoice because Christmas is near. This Homily was delivered in St. Joseph's Christchurch in December 2016.

There are some wonderful characters in the Advent Liturgy, but none as significant as John the Baptist. He is the one who points Jesus out with the words: "Behold the Lamb" of God. He is the last of the Prophets of the Hebrew Scriptures and he is a radical prophet.

Christmas is a great opportunity for us to point Jesus out to others. The Word 'Christmas' itself is an indication of what is happening. It means the Mass of Christ. I am sometimes amazed that the name 'Christmas' was not dropped, especially at the Reformation because Luther and the Reformers claimed that the Mass was a blasphemous act.

So, let us hype-up the name 'Christmas' as a focus on Jesus. Unlike John the Baptist, you do not need to go into the desert or eat locusts or wear camel skins. Here are a few practical initiatives that have worked for me over the years.

The *Welcome Home* leaflet was one such idea. Many of you have passed those leaflets on to family, neighbours, friends, and work colleagues. Already I have received positive reactions from some people who have received the leaflet. Thanks to those who have done the task. You are John the Baptist pointing others to Jesus.

Another Initiative is the Christingle Celebration, usually held on the Fourth Sunday of Advent. We invited all the parents who had children baptised in the last five years and the parents and children who made their First Holy Communion in the last two years. We also invited all the parents and children from the local Catholic

School. We used the Christingle Celebration because we thought it might be less threatening than Mass. Whatever we do, we need to show that coming to Church is a good experience for young and old alike.

You would expect somebody to speak to you, to make you welcome. You might even have people get up to let you sit down.

Welcoming people is not just confined to those wonderful people who give out the Hymn Books at the back of the Church. Hospitality belongs to us all.

I wanted the community to be alive and thriving with a love for the Lord which is automatically transferred to those who come their way. If everyone is aware that the person sitting next to them at Christmas might well be a nervous wreck because it is not easy to come to Church, it would make a difference to that person's life.

Like John the Baptist, we have received a wonderful gift and it becomes a gift when we give it away and can say: "Behold the Lamb of God".

Browsing the World Wide Web for Christmas

With Papal backing, the internet is a powerful tool for spreading the Gospel. It can also be a useful aid to inspiration and reflection on specific issues, such as those that occupy the minds and hearts of the faithful during the four weeks of Advent which lead to the celebration of the birth of Christ.

Some serious-minded people claim that the World Wide Web has been as revolutionary for Christianity today as the introduction of the printing press to Europe was in the fifteenth century. In May 2009, Pope Benedict XVI said we should employ these new technologies to make the Gospel known, so that the good news of God's infinite love for all people will resound in new ways across our technological world.

Bishop Arthur Roche of Leeds went on to say that few of us could ever have imagined how the world of communication would develop and what new opportunities there would be to proclaim the Gospel of Christ in our day. The internet, he said, is one of the greatest tools at our disposal today.

Those words of endorsement sent me in search of how I could prepare personally for Christmas. I discovered a wealth of beautiful resources that enriched my Advent journey. The following web pages are my chosen few from countless internet sites that are available free at the press of a button.

Some are blog/*Facebook* friendly. Some are designed to be used with other people, your family, or fellow parishioners, while others are for private use, in the same way that one can make a private retreat. It is worth viewing the sites to get a taste of what is available; and encourage people to choose one for their spiritual journey towards the Feast of the Nativity – suggesting that they should not be afraid to interact with what is on the screen.

For example, **www.faith-at-home.com** is exactly what it says. This is ideal for parents and children working together in the family setting, offering ideas for family rituals, excellent catechesis on the "why" and "how" we do things for Christmas. For example, the family can make a Nativity scene for the sitting room, select music, or even have a family Nativity play about the Holy Family in Bethlehem. The caption on the page is very catchy: "Explore and enjoy your faith with your kids".

The definitive guide to Advent and Christmas on **www.osv.com** is most certainly comprehensive enough to include 10 ways on how to get more out of Advent. There is an explanation of Advent and its traditions. It highlights the rich symbols of the season: the Jesse Tree, the Advent wreath, the Advent calendar, the Advent chain and much more. There is a weekly introduction to the readings for Advent. These reflections are brief enough for the priest to share with the weekday congregation as an introduction to the liturgy for the week. Finally, there is something on the O Antiphons for the special octave days leading up to Christmas.

A good source of prayer is www.wellsprings.org.uk. It has nourished my faith journey with gems for many years. It was created by Catherine McElhinney and Kathryn Turner in 1994; but every year there is something new. It contains material that can be used for Advent liturgies; the schemes are completely worked through (although, of course, it can be adapted for local use).

For example, some of the liturgies that can be included for parish groups are "Angel Voices", "Come Lord Jesus" and "Travelling Nativity". One of the oldest and best-known spiritual sites on the internet is **www.sacredspace.ie**. Many people use it for their daily prayer; it is profoundly prayerful. There is a different prayer for each day, divided into six sections that run like this: presence, freedom, consciousness, Word of God, conversion, and conclusion.

People are invited to work through all six stages at their own pace; but you get the impression that the designer of this site invites you to slow down and take things easy. Even the change of the page takes a moment, creating a pause that gives you time to ponder and to contemplate the exercise you are involved in. There are other pages on the *Sacred Space* site too. "Living Space" offers a commentary on the readings for every day of Advent, inviting the user into reflection – and offering priests something they can use for their reflections on the readings at Mass.

Finally, there is a feedback page. Some of the views from people all over the world are very inspiring. This entire site is easy to navigate, and all the usual share facilities are available.

By far the most challenging web page for all kinds of reasons is **www.cafod.org.uk** interactive-advent-calendar. The Advent calendar consists of opening a window for each day of Advent. I could not resist opening everyone (for the purposes of this article, of course). Inside each window there is a challenge that appears to get bigger as you get closer to Christmas. The issues highlighted are real, as are the pictures of real people.

The whole project is as much about giving as it is receiving. You find children wanting to do sponsored runs because they want children on the other side of the world to be fed, and to have a school or a hospital. There is a real solidarity of humankind within the windows of this calendar. In a beautiful way, it takes account of the feast days in Advent as well as a major preoccupation of most people – shopping. This Advent calendar could be amazingly effective in the classroom, with a different child opening the window for the given day but the whole class being involved in the suggested exercise. It can also be used in the Children's Liturgy of the Word during Sunday Mass or downloaded for every family in the parish. If it is used in all three locations then there is a harmonious solidarity with people less well off than us that involves the home, the school and the parish.

These are some of the examples of what the internet offers. The God of the Incarnation is calling us to communicate with each other. Of course, the Incarnation of Jesus is the greatest form of communication humans have ever experienced.

(Citation: GRUFFERTY, T. November 2011. *The Tablet.*)

Christmas Traditions

Many of our famous Christmas traditions have their origins in England. In 1372 we find a Franciscan friar Johan de Grimestone with a carol named "Lullay, lullay, as I lay on Yoolis night". The story tells of a mother rocking her son to sleep as she sings of the events which led up to his birth. Other carols were to follow in a similar fashion, so we have the lively 15th century carol, "Nova, Nova" which tells the story of the Annunciation. The most famous medieval English Christmas Carol called the "Coventry Carol" is taken from a 15th century play about the slaughter of the Holy Innocents.

The twelve days of Christmas from Christmas Day until the Feast of Epiphany, January 6th were special rest days when all manual work was suspended. I wonder what our politicians would say if all Christians were to down tools for the twelve days of Christmas. All these days were marked with dinners, carol singing, dances and plays.

In post-Reformation England, there were strong moves to banish all Christmas traditions. The Puritans managed to close all churches on Christmas Day while shops remained in business. Meanwhile the Catholics taught the Catechism in allegory fashion with "The 12 days of Christmas".

Each item has a clever symbolic imagery, the partridge stands for one God, the two turtledoves are the Old and New Testaments, the three French hens are the Trinity, the four calling birds are the four Gospels and so on to include the seven Sacraments, the Ten Commandments and the twelve articles of the Apostles' Creed.

The prohibitions of the Puritans were only lifted when King Charles II came to the throne in 1660. But it took another two hundred years for all the Christmas Traditions to recover. In subsequent centuries more were added or came into vogue, the red robin, holly, and ivy. The first Christmas card appeared in 1843 and the first Christmas tree arrived in England in the1870's. Queen Victoria and Prince Albert made the card and the Christmas tree famous. So much so that the idea spread around the world.

One of England's most famous traditions only began in 1918. "The Festival of Nine Lessons and Carols" takes place at 3 p.m. in the Chapel of King's College Cambridge. This Anglican Service emulates the Catholic Office of Matins.

There is room for more traditions if only to remind us of the warmth and beauty of Christ born in love for the whole of mankind.

Christmas and Posh Spice

Welcome to Christmas this year and welcome especially to this Parish Community. I hope that you have many blessings during these incredibly special festive days. I was in company a few nights ago. I got talking to a younger version of 'Posh Spice'. She asked what I would be doing during Christmas. When I told her that I would spend a great deal of Christmas Eve and Christmas morning in Church, she laughed and said, 'how strange'. This extremely attractive young woman did not connect the birth of Jesus with anything we might do in church. The Mass of Christ or Christmas had no bearing on Bethlehem.

Ignorance of the real Christmas story might easily be more widespread than we think. We assume that people might sing beautiful lyrics in our Christmas Carols without having a clue about their meaning. I found it refreshing to have to explain in the simplest of English the meaning of the Incarnation although I did not use that big word.

Jesus was the Son of God, promised as the Saviour of the world for generations. He was born in a stable in Bethlehem about 2000 years ago. Shepherds and Wise Men came to the stable to rejoice with Mary and Joseph. They acknowledged Jesus as the Saviour. Oh, there might have been animals in the stable! When Jesus grew up, He did wonderful things for people and He was a great preacher. He was crucified for our sins at the age of 33 and three days later, He rose from the dead. Christians believe that Jesus continues to save us from our sins. God became one of us, God has kissed humankind.

The young woman sat there in amazement. I was equally astonished by that fact that she must have spent her short life in a capsule without any interaction with Christians. It is possible that we ourselves do not connect our celebrations today with the birth of Jesus in Bethlehem.

Whatever we understand about the birth of Jesus, the fundamental truth is that God has immersed Himself in our world. He is part of the mess. In fact, He comes to clear and repair the mess. He brings mystery, love, and good will to all this Christmas Day. We should not underestimate His profound love for each one of us.

If I mention that word 'Incarnation' again, you, dear reader, at least understand its full implications while my casual raving beauty is still wondering about the sheep, the smell of hay and the sight of cow dung in the presence of an incredibly special baby whose birthday is December 25th.

Incidentally, as I left the party, I overheard a very

excited Posh Spice look-alike expound on the real meaning of Christmas to a younger version of Becks. I heard her use the words 'God has kissed humankind'. I thought to myself as I got into my little car, 'you only need to tell the real story to one person'.

A Favourite Nativity Artwork

Figure 1   *Tondo Doni* by Michelangelo

The Nativity of Jesus must be the greatest subject of all religious paintings in history.   In fact, the first known painting belongs to the 4th century. If you examine your Christmas cards, those that you send and receive, you may well be surprised about the number of Nativity scenes.   Some will be by famous artists especially belonging to the Renaissance period.

I have a good six to eight famous works of art that have become my favourite depictions of the Birth of Jesus in Bethlehem.   Among these is Michelangelo's 'Tondo Doni' in the Uffizi in Florence.

It is still in its original frame which creates its own speculation that the frame is as equally treasured as the painting itself.

The background is a rural scene with Mary as the prominent figure in the composition. She sits directly on the grass as if to say the Incarnation is an earthy event. Notice the nakedness of Mary's right foot, which is the same message. But that is not all. Mary sits between the legs of St. Joseph. Michelangelo is inviting us to see a throne, take a step back and you see both sides of the magnificent chair.

There is speculation also about whether Mary is handing the baby Jesus to St. Joseph or the other way round. I think it's the former, as the Mother gives her child for the salvation of the world. Michelangelo knew his scriptures and he crams as much as possible into his paintings.

St Joseph is much older than you would expect but notice his position. This is most unusual for a Renaissance painter as Joseph is usually positioned in a humbler place. For Michelangelo, Joseph is the Guardian, the Protector of the Holy Family.

There is also the question of the nude figures in the background. Is the great painter inviting us to see the nakedness of the old Adam in the Garden of Eden with the new Adam in Jesus?

"The first man, Adam, became a living being the last Adam became a life-giving spirit". (1 Corinthians 15:45).

Thanks to Paul, he echoes the whole entire creation story right up to you, who is now looking at this great work of art. Stay with it for as long as you like. Try to get behind the images, especially of Jesus, Mary and Joseph. As a real Christmas present, place yourself, and those you love into this famous work of Art.

(GRUFFERTY, T. April – June 2017. *Portsmouth People*)

Figure 2 The Manger and the Cross by Beate Heinen

I was at Notre Dame de Paris. At 9.30a.m. I was joined by a group of about 400 people queueing to get inside the famous building. Once inside, it became instantly clear that the greater part of the crowd gathered to gaze at the three Rose Windows in the building. These windows must be the greatest masterpieces in glass in the whole world. People of all religions and none, were transfixed as they absorbed the vibrant colours. In many ways, this is a powerful way of prayer. As I looked at these people, I could see immediately that some, if not all, were praying.

Of course, we have prayed with images for centuries, and we are sometimes ridiculed for it, the Reformers and the iconoclastic movement being two examples of those who did so. I would like to invite you to pray this Christmas with this painting. Mary Huntley, who is a friend, sent me this Christmas card many years ago. From the moment I first saw it, I loved the symbolism and I have kept the card in my treasure chest. It is by a German artist called Beate Heinen who created the work in 1986.

Before you read any further, just spend a few minutes looking at what the artist has done. Pause for a little while. Now read the Nativity Story, as told in Luke's Gospel (2:1-20) very carefully. Stop to ponder whenever you wish. Now look again at the painting. Your eyes are immediately drawn to the nativity scene. It is small and compact and easy on the eye. Like most nativity scenes, you are drawn to the crib. Hold on to some of the things that Luke has just said to you personally. Notice that the scene is full. Mary is in blue as you would expect, Joseph is dressed in brown. Mary lovingly touches the hand of her Son. Look at Jesus. The crib is a marble coffin, which comes as a shock. But all will be made clear shortly.

Imagine you have the powers of a panoramic photo lens and move your eyes out to capture what the artist really wants you to see. The immediate surroundings are full of vegetation, colour and vibrancy. This is strangely unseasonal for the middle of winter in the Northern Hemisphere.

The first thoughts that came to my mind were that there could be some surprises in store in this painting. In the wider panorama, we have winter when it should be spring. Here the landscape is cold, bleak with snow and frost. Then you see the three crosses on Calvary …winter has become spring and spring has become winter.

The artist knows only too well that the crib and the cross are integral parts of the same story. Christmas and Good Friday come together. This contradiction leads us to Jesus Himself when He explains the chief reason for the Incarnation. In John's Gospel, Jesus says to Pilate: "I was born for this, I came into the world for this, to bear witness to the truth and all who live by the truth listen to my voice" (John 18:37). Just before His crucifixion, death and resurrection, Jesus takes us to the Christmas Crib. What does Christmas really say to you? How can you pray Christmas? We can only pray Christmas in the context of Calvary, and at the empty tomb. The crib is full, the tomb is empty. There is a powerful and inseparable correlation between the two places.

Now look at the painting again. Did you notice the Road of Life? There are three people on it, and I do not know who they are. Peter, James, and John, perhaps? They were with Jesus at least on Mount Tabor and in the Garden of Gethsemane, so why not here?

But I would really like to think these are three women for they look like women. Mary the Mother of Jesus, His great friend Mary of Magdala and Mary of Cleopas in John 19:25

All three are directly connected with Christmas and Easter. Mary as Mother is central to the crib, Mary Magdala is central to the crucifixion and Mary of Cleopas is engaged directly too.

But let me lead you into THE MOST PROFOUND contemplation ---the three people are us. You and me on the road of life between birth, death, and the RESURRECTION!

A Christmas Present - A Tablecloth

I have no idea where this story came from. When I was a seminarian in All Hallows College in Dublin, we got very lucrative jobs in New York City for three months during the summer. This was a great opportunity to visit two uncles on my mother's side who had spent nearly all their lives in or near the Big Apple. Eddie and his wife Eileen owned an off License (called a 'liquor store') in Brooklyn. Eileen gave me a copy of this story as she firmly said: "This will be far more enlightening than all that stuff you are learning in the Seminary."

A new priest was appointed to a new parish in downtown Brooklyn. The parish church was in a complete mess. He resolved to have the place ready for Midnight Mass. He and his parishioners worked hard in the run-up to Christmas. Nobody could get rid of a great big black mark on the back wall of the Church. Many people had tried but it could not be removed.

A few days before Christmas, the priest was in the flea market when he saw a crocheted tablecloth with fine colours and a Cross right in the centre of the tablecloth. It was just the right size to cover the black mark on the Sanctuary Wall, so He bought it. As he returned to the presbytery, he noticed a woman running for a bus which she missed. They chatted and he invited her to wait in the church for the next bus which was 20 minutes later. He began to hang the tablecloth, when suddenly he saw the woman walk up the aisle. She was as white as a sheet.

She asked the priest where he got the tablecloth. When he explained that he had just bought it in the market, she asked him to check the lower right-hand corner for the initials EBG. These were the initials of the woman who had made the tablecloth in Austria 35 years before. She went on to say before the war she and her husband were well-to-do people in Austria. They were forced to leave, but her husband insisted that she leave first, and he would follow a week later. She never saw her home or her husband again.

Instead of allowing the woman to take the bus, the priest decided to give her a lift home. Christmas Midnight Mass came. They had a great celebration and the priest greeted the people as they left Midnight Mass. When he came back into the church, he noticed an old man starring at the tablecloth. The old man asked the priest where he had got the tablecloth because it was identical to one his wife made in Austria 35 years before. When the Nazis came, he insisted that his wife should flee, and he would follow. He was arrested and imprisoned for many years but, after the war, he travelled to America to look for his wife. He never did find her as she must have changed her name. The priest invited the old man to take a trip with him then and there. He retraced his journey to EBG and there was the greatest reunion you can ever imagine.

All due to a tablecloth! (Incidentally, I returned to All Hallows that Autumn with a new outlook on life in a lockdown institution, but more significantly in my future as a priest!)

A Parish Swap

I feel obliged to include something about Australia in this publication. In 1995, I swapped parishes with Fr Des Magennis in Melbourne for a whole twelve months. It was the greatest sabbatical ever as the lay people in both parishes expected their visiting priest to relax and enjoy a different culture. Both Des and I shared the same wonderful ministry from lay people who rose to the occasion and not only encouraged us but enabled us to explore the natives. I am incredibly grateful to Bishop Crispian Hollis for his enthusiastic support of the idea. A few years later we did a much shorter exchange when I spent three months in the lovely gold-rush town of Castlemaine on the Murray. I am also grateful to the people of Havant and Emsworth for their warm welcome of the Ozzie Priest with an Irish name.

Sydney Opera House

A Blessing for New Year's Day

In 2007, I gave a copy of the following Blessing to everyone in the parish. Some people used it throughout the year. We also used it in place of a homily on New Year's Day.

When the month of your birth is called, come forward and light your candle.

Then pray the response which is the same for all 12 months

The idea is taken from *Intercom* and extended by T Grufferty Dec 2001.

New Year's Day Blessing

JANUARY   The month of new promises, new beginnings, and prayers for Christian Unity

Walk with us closely, Lord.

FEBRUARY   The month for Ash Wednesday and Lenten Renewal

Walk closely with us, Lord.

MARCH   The month of our Patron Saint, Holy Thursday, Good Friday and Easter with new Faith and New Life

Walk closely with us, Lord.

APRIL   The month of new flowers, lambs, and new green grass

Walk closely with us, Lord.

MAY   The month of Mary, the Ascension, the Feasts of Pentecost, the most Holy Trinity and Corpus Christi

Walk closely with us, Lord.

JUNE   The month of the Sacred Heart, first Holy Communions, the feasts of Saints John Fisher and Thomas More, Peter and Paul

Walk closely with us, Lord.

JULY   The month of school holidays and summer rains

Walk closely with us, Lord.

AUGUST   The month of harvest and of the feasts of the Transfiguration and the Assumption

Walk closely with us, Lord.

SEPTEMBER The month of fruits, new schools, and St. Michael

Walk closely with us, Lord.

OCTOBER   The month of the Holy Rosary, Family Fast Day

Walk closely with us, Lord.

NOVEMBER   The month of All Saints, Holy Souls and Remembrance.

Walk closely with us, Lord.

DECEMBER   The month of preparations and waiting, and a time for the Saviour.
Walk closely with us, Lord

A PRAYER

My life is a gift given, not in years,

but a day at a time.

This day the Lord has made for me.

He has planned it to be the most important day of my life.

Last year has gone, never to return.

I do not worry about what is gone.

I leave it in the hands of the Lord.

Tomorrow is not yet and it holds God's secrets.

Only today is mine.

It is beautifully arranged by God.

In thanksgiving, I now offer myself to Him,

My prayers, my works, my joys and sorrows, my hopes, and my sufferings.

Dear Lord, accept it graciously.

Lent

Fasting from bad things: -

Gossip, Complaining, calling people names, Negativity, Judging people, Arguing, Lying, Being angry, Being greedy

Fasting from 'good' things: -

Television, *Facebook*, Fizzy drinks, Chocolate, Sweets, Junk food, Coffee, Cream and Sugar, Sarcasm, Chewing gum, Idle curiosity.

Instead….

❖ Read a chapter of the Bible each day.

❖ Fast from something especially if you enjoy it.

❖ Give your mum and dad a hug.

❖ Tell your brother or your sister that you appreciate what they **do** for you. Give somebody in your class a word of praise, especially when they do something well.

❖ Help somebody on the bus.

❖ March 25 is the feast day of the Annunciation. April 1 is called 'All Fool's Day' but do not make a fool of anybody who is vulnerable.

❖ Go to Mass on all the Sundays of Lent. Make a special point of celebrating Holy Week by attending Mass on Palm Sunday.

- ❖ Displaying your palm cross in your room.
- ❖ Fast from judging others. Feast on Christ living in them.
- ❖ Fast from Darkness. Feast on the reality of light
- ❖ Fast from anger. Feast on patience
- ❖ Fast from bitterness. Feast on forgiveness
- ❖ Fast from emphasis on difference. Feast on the unity of life.
- ❖ Fast from thoughts of sickness. Feast on the healing hand of God.
- ❖ Fast from worry. Feast on the providence of God.
- ❖ Fast from pessimism. Feast on optimism
- ❖ Fast from negatives. Feast on the affirmative.
- ❖ Fast from complaining. Feast on appreciation.
- ❖ Fast from pressures. Feast on reflective quietness.
- ❖ Fast from gossip. Feast on the facts.
- ❖ Fast from problems you cannot solve. Feast on prayers that achieve.
- ❖ Fast from self-pity. Feast on compassion for others.
- ❖ Fast from apathy. Feast on enthusiasm.
- ❖ Fast from laziness. Feast on doing it yourself.
- ❖ Fast from criticism. Feast on praise for effort.

Lent towards Easter Tablet Lenten Treasure

A journey towards the Resurrection
St. John Chrysostom gives a wonderful reason why we do extra exercises during Lent.

He says that everything we do for Lent should enable us to partake more fully in the Eucharist. We pray, we fast and give alms because we recognise the Risen Lord in the breaking of bread. With that understanding of our journey towards Easter, I share with you the following three suggestions for improving your spiritual journey towards renewing your faith in the Resurrection.

The first exercise is best done with fellow Christians; the second and third can either be done in private or with other people in your Parish. In our Parish, we have done 'The York Course' for many years. We have several ecumenical groups in the area. The dynamic of this course is the essence of simplicity: refreshments, prayer, listening to the reflections on CD, and following the same in the Booklet, then discussion on the theme of the session.

The Course for 2012 is called 'Handing on the Torch' and the speakers include *The Tablet*'s very own Clifford Longley JP, Rachel Lampard, Archbishop John Sentamu, and Bishop Graham Gray. The four speakers address issues about a Church that might be beleaguered; about whether we live in a Christian country; about secular society; competing Creeds; and handing on the torch.

The meetings spread over the five weeks of Lent, are ecumenical, and last for one hour. We have our meetings on different days and times, to offer as many people as possible the opportunity to participate. The material is flexible and works best when used ecumenically, with a certain amount of silence.

This is a great opportunity to share the strengths of

the prayer life of each participating individual, especially if a different person is asked to lead the prayer section each week.

To find out more contact www.yorkcourses.co.uk

Recently when I was travelling on the 06.24 train from Waterloo to Havant, the woman sitting beside me was using a tablet computer (no relation). The machine really grabbed my attention when I realised that the woman was praying Evening Prayer from the Breviary. When it was clear that she had finished, we got talking about prayer in public places. She introduced me to http://onlineministries.creighton.edu/

This prayer site comes from the Jesuit University of Creighton in Nebraska. It must be one of the most powerful prayer sites in the world. Without doubt, the Jesuits are on the front line of prayer ministries. The site has multi links, dealing with every aspect of prayer, from retreats to Stations of the Cross, to daily reflections.

My interest is in the latter. Over 50 members of staff prepare daily reflections which mean that each day there is a different writer. The reflection is based on the Readings of the Day. Having prayed through the reflection, there is an opportunity to ponder, and you can even reply to the writer. This makes the site interactive.

I have experimented with this by doing the exercise before Mass. I can assure you that it makes an enormous difference to my celebration of the daily Eucharist. What about recommending this for all our Readers and Eucharistic Ministers, at least on Sundays?

There are days when it offers remarkable insights into the scriptures. The use of this site by several parishioners individually and collectively could be a wonderful opportunity for growth in parish renewal. A suggestion to hold a weekly parish meeting of all those doing the exercise would be a real benefit to see how parishioners are making progress.

The whole site is rich with spiritual treasures, nearly all of which can be downloaded to your PC or handheld device. For Lent there is a section called 'Choosing Lent/Acting Lent' with different headings including one named "Symbols in the Home". The practice of having religious symbols has almost disappeared from our homes and even our Catholic Schools.

The site recommends that we can easily redress the balance by displaying a crucifix as a powerful reminder of the love of the crucified Lord for us. A bowl of sand reminds us that we are in the desert with the Lord in all the temptations of the modern age. Placing a candle on the dinner table can be a great sign that we share in the light of Christ.

This could be linked to the Paschal Candle in Church at the Easter Vigil and beyond. Why not encourage families to have their own Easter Candle at home? The greatest symbol must be the Bible, open and on display, for all to see that we are guided by the Word. The site suggests that the family could discuss these symbols at mealtimes during Lent.

There are many other practical ideas on how to make family life operate more smoothly, even to one family member being responsible for putting out the rubbish!

The Lenten Companion of the 'Magnificat' (www.magnificat.com) is well worth a browse if for no other reason than that it contains explanations of several Lenten Traditions from around the world. I especially liked James Monti's description 'A Portuguese Journey to Easter'. There are many traditions that could be easily incorporated into the practices of faith communities in our Pastoral Areas. If your parish has Eucharistic Adoration, why not move Exposition around the neighbouring parishes especially if they do not have Eucharistic

Adoration.

On Holy Thursday in the Archdiocese of Barga, they have a unique rite. With permission from the Vatican, there is 'The Rite of Braga' in which the Archbishop washes the feet of the people in a ceremony entirely outside of Mass.

There is a short section at the end with special prayers and a brief Stations of the Cross. If you seek a new motivation to do the Stations of the Cross you could do no better than pray the Stations with these words, 'the Way of the Cross is a school of inner depth and maturity, a school for interiority and consolation, an examination of conscience, for conversion, a disturbing experience that knocks on the door of my heart, that obliges me to know myself better and become a better person'
(Pope Benedict XVI).

This publication also has a daily reflection for each day of Lent. The reflection leads into a short prayer and suggested penance. All three could be used by the priest as part of the daily Eucharist in the parish. The publication does not take account of the beautiful feast days we have in Lent, but that might be since it is a 'companion' to the main publication. Using this little treasure daily could easily form and focus your spiritual journey towards Easter, filling you with a new conviction of the Risen Lord among us.

(Citation: GRUFFERTY, T. February 2012. *The Tablet.*)

Lent on the Celluloid Way

Still image from *The Way* (2010) directed by Emilio Estevez and starring Martin Sheen.

This Lent consider making a journey of faith on the route to Santiago de Compostela. Without leaving home, you can walk with others, join with them in prayer, and share bread and Rioja wine, guided by the narrative of an extraordinary movie called "The Way" and a book called *The Long Road to Heaven* by Tim Heaton. Your Christian way of life will be challenged and nourished by the wisdom of the centuries. The film, which was directed and written by Emilio Estevez, is about Tom, an American doctor, played by Martin Sheen, who comes to Europe because his son has tragically died on the Way of St James, the pilgrim route in the Pyrenees that leads to the Apostle's shrine in Santiago de Compostela. The angry and irascible ophthalmologist has his son's body cremated and decides to finish the Camino, in his son's memory and on his son's behalf, by carrying his ashes to Santiago. Little by little, Sheen is drawn into a personal encounter with himself and with what is important in life.

As in life, nobody reaches their destiny without the

help of others. As our journey progresses, we need the constant assurance that we are saved from sin, as promised by the Lord himself. Tom sets out on his journey with a heavy heart and a grieving mind.

In real life, Martin Sheen was, at the time of filming, a lapsed Catholic, but as the film progresses you can see his character grow in faith. The death of Daniel becomes a blessing for the present and an inspiration for the future, making it possible for all the pilgrims to cope with anything the Camino might throw at them. At first, there are only two people on the journey, a selfish father with the ashes of his misunderstood son, who appears mysteriously on the journey. But, surprise, surprise God and other people are on the road too. The footprints of others begin to intrude and liven up the journey. The stubborn father resists the intrusion from outsiders.

In his book, Tim Heaton maintains that we cannot do such a journey without breaking bread <u>together</u>. In sharing bread and wine, we discover our dependence on others, but equally, their dependence on us. Only then does the road ahead get exciting; only then can we place one foot in front of the other. So, now there are six very different characters on the road to Heaven. All these characters can be found in every parish. Every community has the equivalent of the jovial Dutchman who is trapped in a loveless marriage, or Sarah the Canadian, who is now divorced from an abusive husband. Sarah had an abortion because she feared that the same abuse would happen to her child. There is Jack, an Irish travel writer with numerous chips on both shoulders, particularly caused by the Troubles in his country. This character can be found in parish life too. Finally, there is Daniel, Tom's son, who appears in flashbacks in the film. His presence is deeply spiritual. Daniel is played by Sheen's own son and the film's director, which adds another dimension. Daniel becomes an influence on, and the conscience of, the other five pilgrims.

But ironically, there is no way that God finds them. Taking part in a Lent course like this to allow God to find us can easily become a life-changing experience. A group, the DVD and the book are all essential for this pilgrimage, which can take place with a small group in someone's home or with small or large groups in the parish.

Each session begins with a clip of the film followed by the question for the given week. Season the session with prayers from Bonhoeffer's "Prayers for fellow-Prisoners, Christmas 1943" in *Letters and Prayers from Prison* and finish it off with the breaking of bread for each other and a glass of Rioja which is actually a region on the Camino.

The first question asks the pilgrims what we are saved from. It is easy enough to answer that we are saved from sin. But how many Christians look as if they are forgiven? The group could easily spend the whole of Lent exploring the God of the second chance. For me, one of the great revelations was that in one Lent Group I did this with at least three parents of a group of 20 had lost children. It was that issue that echoed in the lives of all those who took part.

(Citation: GRUFFERTY, T. March 2014. *The Tablet*.)

Third Sunday of Lent - Mothering Sunday

We have a great devotion to Mary the Mother of Jesus, and rightly so. In Liturgical terms, we need to find ways to pay tribute to all the Mothers and Grandmothers in the Church pews. We give them flowers on this day, but we miss an opportunity to pay tribute to their magnanimity and generosity in the home, in the school and in the parish. Parish life would be decimated without the pastoral generosity of all women and mothers.

The Images of Mothers

4 YEARS OF AGE - My Mummy can do anything!

8 YEARS OF AGE - My Mum knows a lot! A whole lot!

12 YEARS OF AGE - My Mother does not know everything!

14 YEARS OF AGE - My Mother? She would not have a clue.

16 YEARS OF AGE - Mum? She is so five minutes ago.

18 YEARS OF AGE - That old woman? She is way out of date!

25 YEARS OF AGE - Well, she might know a little bit about it!

35 YEARS OF AGE - Before we decide, let us get Mum's opinion.

45 YEARS OF AGE - Wonder what Mum would have thought about it?

65 YEARS OF AGE - Wish I could talk it over with Mum.

The Beauty of a Woman

The beauty of a woman is not in the clothes she wears, the figure she carries, or the way she combs her hair.

The beauty of a woman must be seen from in her eyes,

Because that is the doorway to her heart,

The place where love resides.

The beauty of a woman is not in a facial mole,

But true beauty in a woman is reflected in her soul.

It is the caring that she lovingly gives, the passion that she shows,

and the beauty of a woman with passing years only grows!

(Anon)

Wednesday of Easter Week and the Third Sunday of Easter.

Figure 3 Jesus and the Breaking of Bread
Caravaggio

Praying with Caravaggio for the Easter Season

Dear Reader, I alert you to the Gospel for Wednesday of Easter Week and for the Third Sunday of Easter. The story of the two disciples on the Road to Emmaus is a profound story of great importance, not only for Cleopas and his companion but for all of us who meet Jesus in the Breaking of Bread. Although Mark mentions the meeting very briefly in 16:12, we find the whole story only in Luke. William Barclay in his commentary on the Gospel of Luke says that the Christian never walks into the sunset but always to the sunrise. Also, we should never forget that, for centuries, Mass was known as 'the breaking of Bread', on the strength of this story. I personally love the suggestion that the companion of Cleopas was his wife.

As a believer in the Lord, meeting us in the breaking of Bread, I would like to invite you to read, contemplate and prayer the Gospel story in a different way this year. First read the Gospel slowly for three days during the octave of Easter, perhaps in three parts. Do this in the morning so that you can be mindful of the events and the words in the story for the rest of that day.

It would be great if you could attend Mass on Wednesday so that you hear the Gospel proclaimed within the Eucharist itself. Make sure you place yourself in one of the following characters as found in this great paining of Caravaggio. In 1601, Ciriaco Mattei commissioned Caravaggio to paint this masterpiece. Mattei had a brother who was a cardinal and they were a rich noble family. We are lucky in this country because the painting is displayed in the National Gallery in London (Room 31).

I often go there just to soak up the atmosphere. It is noticeable that the painting attracts a wide variety of people including school children out for the day. It is also particularly useful to listen to the guide explain the story to the children. Now make the masterpiece personal to you. Look at the characters with the intention to make yourself present. Look at Jesus. He does not have a beard which was most unusual 400 years ago. This is the face of a man who has not suffered the crucifixion of only a few days ago. This is the New Christ of the Resurrection. There is youthfulness and vibrancy in the face. This is life and life in abundance. Jesus is using both hands to bless. With the right hand, he blesses the disciples and with the left hand he blesses the bread.

There are three pieces of bread on the table. A carafe of wine, as you would expect. The exotic fruits are interesting because these would not be found in springtime, but only in the Autumn. I wonder what Caravaggio was saying there. Also notice that the bowl of fruit is lilting precariously towards the edge of the table.

The reaction of Cleopas and his companion is my favourite part of the painting. One stretches out his arms in disbelief. Notice the Camino shell as the sign of the universal pilgrimage. The other one is about to leave the table because he is in a state of shock. Notice the hole in the elbow of his garment. Perhaps the bowl of fruit is lilting over too in disbelief.

Then there is the innkeeper who wears a Muslim head covering. He is non-plussed. I wonder if he stands for all the unbelievers, atheists and agnostics Caravaggio met on his travels. Finally, look at the source of light which enables us to see the details. Caravaggio was revolutionary in his use of light and it would not surprise me that he is telling us that Jesus is the light of the world.

Stay with the painting if you like, but when you have finished, read the Gospel story again, preferably in three parts. Then, when you are at Mass next time, make a real effort to recognise Jesus in the Breaking of the Bread.

May - "Rosary on the Coast"

This was an initiative of the laity and proved remarkably successful in Ireland and Poland. It came to Great Britain big time on 29 April 2018. The three intentions for prayer could not have been greater - world peace, the whole of life and greater faith. Without a shadow of doubt, Catholics gathering in any public place are a powerful witness to our faith and one that is noticed. I observed several people, dog walkers included, acknowledge our prayerful presence as we gathered in Stokes Bay, some stopped to listen to what was going on.

But another thoughtful product of the exercise belonged to those who took part. This was in many ways a mini pilgrimage as we moved out of our comfort zone to worship, praise, and prayer in a completely different environment than normal.

There were a variety of venues across the Solent Coast from Bournemouth to the walls of Portsmouth City. The Prayer had an ecumenical dimension too as Catholics gathered in St. Mary's Anglican Church in Portchester. Those who gathered there for prayer were not only praying with the thousands around the coast of Britain, all at the same time, but also with those from Roman times, through the Middle Ages right up to 29 April.

Getting there was an effort because the weather was cold. Staying the course also demanded effort as we were exposed to a very cold breeze. These negatives were richly compensated for by what I call "Prayers across the Solent".

I thought that this was a new face of the Church, ordinary people gathered in prayer, ordinary people freezing from the Solent winds but willing to stay the course as we contemplated the glorious mysteries. For me personally, the Resurrection, Ascension and the Descent of the Holy Spirit took on a completely different perception as we raised our minds and hearts across the Solent. Even in the wind and the cloud, Christ's glory became our glory and the gifts of the Holy Spirit became our gifts as we returned home.

This initiative was a new way of praying and it inspired me to search for new ways to pray with imagination, with vision, with image but especially nature and the sea. When you think about the famous places of prayer, many are within easy reach of the sea, like Lindisfarne and Iona.

(Citation: GRUFFERTY, T. July 2018. *Portsmouth People*)

Mindfulness on the Feast of the Ascension

Many years ago, I had arranged to meet a friend in Leicester Square in London. With half an hour to spare, I visited Notre Dame de France Church, just off the Square. I was overwhelmed to find an art exhibition by Elisabeth Wang. Once I met my friend, we both returned to the Church to view the paintings in greater detail. I have been astonished by this modern artist ever since that day.

Elizabeth Wang was born in 1942 and received into the Catholic Church in 1968. She was an artist, housewife and mother. She spent much of her life writing and speaking about prayer and the Catholic Faith. She was involved in the life of her home parish of Our Lady of Lourdes, Harpenden, particularly as a catechist.

Her children are grown-up, and her son Stephen is a priest in Westminster Diocese. She exhibited at the Royal Academy, and the Royal Institute of Painters in Watercolours. She had solo exhibitions of religious work at Westminster Cathedral, the Bar Convent Museum (York), the Conference Rooms at St Paul's Bookshop, and at Notre Dame de France Church, London. Many of her paintings are published side-by-side with her religious writings. Elizabeth Wang is the founder of Radiant Light, a movement within the Catholic Church which seeks to encourage people to grow in holiness by believing and living the Catholic faith in its fullness. Jesus Christ Himself is 'the radiant light of God's glory' (Heb: 1:3). Every aspect of the work of Radiant Light, is meant to uphold the teaching of the Catholic Church. Visit the webpage of **Radiant Light** and explore the rich contents.

The online Art Gallery contains over 5000 works of art and most have a Christian theme. All the images can be used for non-commercial purposes. There is a wonderful lesson for pupils which can be downloaded by

Teachers. I have found Radiant Light generous to a fault in the contents of its Art Gallery. One of my favourite paintings by Elisabeth Wang is that of The Ascension. See below.

I have examined in detail several famous paintings of the Ascension which are inspirational and prayerful in their own way, but in all cases, there is a vast difference between this world and the world Jesus ascended to. This is often portrayed by light and darkness, i.e. the darkness of this world and the radiant light of the world of the Ascension.

Elisabeth Wang continues the contrast, but with a huge difference. This is not just the Ascension of Jesus; the whole of humanity is Ascending too. This is a communal Ascension. The Risen Lord is surrounded with light and with a large crowd of people approaching from the face of the Earth (notice the Globe). The Father momentarily blocks the way into heaven and the narrative of the narrow door is obvious, "Strive to enter in by the narrow door, for many, I tell you, will seek to enter in, and will not be able" (Luke 13:24).

Notice the power of the left hand of Jesus. This hand points to the multitude This is the hand of hospitality, of friendship and of love. Notice the wound which is a profound clue of salvation for all. The hand with the wound is the great signpost as found in St. John, "Greater love has no man than this, that someone lay down his life for his friends" (John 15:13).

https://radiantlight.org.uk/
(Citation: GRUFFERTY, T. May 2019. *Catholic South West*)

First Novena - Ascension to Pentecost

To embrace the Holy Spirit, doing the original Novena as a parish, praying it over the nine days from the original Feast of the Ascension to Pentecost, can bring a whole new understanding of, and relationship with, the third person of the Trinity. In his book *The Changing Face of Priesthood*, Donald Cozzens tells the story of an ancient traveller who, on leaving a medieval city, meets three men with wheelbarrows. When he asked all three what they were doing, the first, irritated by the question, said: "I am pushing a wheelbarrow full of bricks." The second gave a different answer: "I have a wife and three children. They need food and I am feeding them." The third said: "I am building a great cathedral."

A small group of us decided recently that we are not pushing bricks around; we are building the cathedral of the Body of Christ – and we decided to seek help from the Holy Spirit to celebrate Pentecost this year.

Pentecost is the third greatest feast in the life of the Church. In many ways, it is the Cinderella of feasts because it is the least celebrated. We decided to encourage all our parishioners to pray the Holy Spirit Novena, from the original Feast of the Ascension. When it comes to the Feast of Pentecost itself, we will be pulling out all the stops to have a vibrant and lively liturgy. Every weekend, we celebrate four Masses in the parish. On Pentecost, we have decided to cancel three Masses and have one mega-celebration tonight since the feast provides a vigil celebration. We have invited all our singers and musicians to take part.

This year's Confirmation candidates will be given a special place in this liturgy. The First Holy Communion children, who have already received that Communion, will be invited to attend in their Holy

Communion outfits. This is the parish celebrating all its best features in one annual celebration. If the first Pentecost is about gifts in the Upper Room, so Pentecost in 2011 is about gifts in abundance among all our people.

In addition to Pentecost being a heightened period of prayer in our community, it is also a great feast to acknowledge the gifts as expressed in liturgy and one cannot go wrong with red!

We do need to spend more money on improving the worship ambience. Pentecost is a great opportunity to make a statement that there is something greater here. Following Mass, there will be an American-style potluck supper to which everybody in the parish is invited. There will be games for children provided by the Confirmation candidates. This is one advantage of a late Easter. The meal after the Vigil Mass is intended to be a social extension of the Eucharist. With a small group of enthusiasts, we aim to provide a focus on who we are as a community. In doing so, we acknowledge the giftedness of every member of the community and hope to be able to open people's eyes to who they are and the tasks they have been given by virtue of their baptism.

In place of the Homily and the Prayers of Intercession, we have arranged a combination of both. Each ministry in the parish will be asked to stand. For example, all readers will stand, the community will affirm their final destiny which is the eternal reward for pushing bricks around.

The Holy Spirit Novena is led by different people in the two churches of our parish three times a day for the nine days; and those who cannot be there are invited to pray at home or at work. In addition to the Novena Prayer, we are distributing a leaflet with several other prayers to the Holy Spirit.

This exercise is a powerful Homily, probably the best Homily of the year, because the whole community sees how gifted and how generous it is as the Body of Christ in this place. I know there are people who will be horrified that the Homily is dropped for a para-liturgy, but the Sunday sermon is always more than words.

The church environment will be decorated with lots of colour – the red of Pentecost and the flames of the Holy Spirit everywhere inside the church and outside.

Every baptised person is called on to build a cathedral, enabling every other person to bask in the rays of the Holy Spirit so powerfully manifest at Pentecost.

(Citation: GRUFFERTY, T. June 2011. *The Tablet.*)

Prayers

A Prayer of Reconciliation

Father, I ask you to bless all those from whom I am estranged.

I'm asking you to minister to them at this very moment.

Where I have caused pain, give them your peace and mercy.

Where I am responsible for self-doubt, release a new confidence in your ability to work through them.

When I have generated tiredness, or exhaustion, I ask you to give them understanding, patience and strength.

When I have caused spiritual stagnation, I ask you to renew your intimacy with them.

Where I have created fear, reveal your love, and give them your courage.

If there is a sin blocking them, reveal it and break its hold over their lives.

Bless their finances, give them greater vision, and raise up leaders and friends to support and encourage them.

Give each of them discernment to recognise the evil forces around them and reveal to them the power they have in you to defeat it.

I make this prayer in faith because it is at your altar I will meet the Christ of Bethlehem, the Christ of mercy and the Christ of compassion.

Amen

Praying with the Five Fingers

1.   Your thumb is nearest you. So, begin your prayers by praying for those closest to you. They are the easiest to remember. To pray for our loved ones is, as C. S. Lewis once said, a "sweet duty."

2.   The next finger is the pointing finger. Pray for those who teach, instruct, and heal. This includes teachers, doctors, and ministers. They need support and

wisdom in pointing others in the right direction. Keep them in your prayers.

3.   The next finger is the tallest finger. It reminds us of our leaders. Pray for the leaders of the government, leaders in business and industry, and administrators. These people shape our nation and guide public opinion. They need God's guidance.

4.   The fourth finger is our ring finger. Surprising to many is the fact that this is our weakest finger, as any piano teacher will testify. It should remind us to pray for those who are weak, in trouble or in pain. They need your prayers day and night. You cannot pray too much for them.

5.   And lastly comes our little finger, the smallest finger of all, which is where we should place ourselves in relation to God and others. As the Bible says: "The least shall be the greatest among you" (Luke 9:48). Your pinkie should remind you to pray for yourself. By the time you have prayed for the other four groups, your own needs will be put into proper perspective and you will be able to pray for your needs more effectively.

A Creed to Live By

It is because we are different that each of us is special. Do not set your goals by what other people deem important.

- ❖ Only you know what is best for you.
- ❖ Do not take for granted the things closest to your heart,
- ❖ Cling to them as you would your life, for without them life is meaningless.
- ❖ Do not let your life slip through your fingers by living in the past or in the future, by living your life one day at a time you live all the days of your life.
- ❖ Do not give up when you still have something to give. Nothing is over until the moment you stop trying. You are living do not be afraid to admit that your less than perfect.
- ❖ It is this fragile thread that binds each of us to each other.
- ❖ Do not be afraid to encounter risks. It is by taking chances that we learn how to be brave.
- ❖ Do not shut love out of your life by saying it is impossible to find.
- ❖ The quickest way to receive love is to give love;

- ❖ the fastest way to lose love is to hold it too tightly, and the best way to keep love is to give it wings.
- ❖ Do not dismiss your dreams; to be without your dreams is to be without hope.
- ❖ To be without hope is to be without purpose.
- ❖ Do not run through life so fast that you forget, not only where you have been, but also where you're going.
- ❖ Life is not a race,
- ❖ but a journey to be savoured each step of the way

.

❖Therefore go ...

The Final Account

❖ God will not ask what kind of car you drove, but he will ask how many people you drove who did not have transport.

❖ God will not ask the square footage of your house, but he will ask how many people you welcomed into your home.

❖ God will not ask about the clothes you had in your wardrobe, but he will ask how many others you helped to clothe.

❖ God will not ask about your social status, he really asked how it affected your treatment of others.

❖ God will not ask how many material possessions you had, but he will ask if they dictated your life.

❖ God will not ask what your highest salary was, but he will ask if you compromised your character to obtain it.

❖ God will not ask how much overtime you worked, but he will ask how much overtime truly benefitted your family.

❖ God will not ask how many promotions you received, but he will ask how much encouragement you gave to others.

❖ God will not ask your job title, but he will ask you how you performed it to the best of your ability.

❖ God will not ask what you did to help yourself, but he will ask what you did to help others.

❖ God will not ask how many friends you had, but he will ask how you were a friend to other people.

❖ God will not ask what you did to protect your rights, but he will ask what you did to protect the rights of others.

❖ God will not ask in what neighbourhood, you lived in, but he will ask how you treated your neighbours.

❖ God will not ask the colour of your skin, but he will ask the content of your character.

The Praying Olympics 2012

As a result of the Olympics Games, the connection between sport and faith was highlighted once more. Katie Taylor, the Irish International Boxer and former footballer's deep religious faith comes as no surprise to anyone. The members of her Pentecostal community gathered in prayer before and during her fight. She loves Psalm 18 as she knows that God is her Strength and Rock.

The great Usain Bolt also publicly acknowledges his talents as coming from God. All religions need to affirm those in sport who show their faith in public. As the Olympic Games come to an end and a new season of football begins, here are some people who have impressed me. Many people claim that the local football ground has replaced the local place of worship. Has Stamford Bridge become the Cathedral for London? Footballers have borrowed some rituals from religion; football has its liturgical colours; the players might be the gods, while those in the stands used to sit in the pews. The congregation has its favourite hymns and there is wonderful fellowship on the terraces. There is also something new happening among the players and we Christians would be foolish not to acknowledge it.

There is an increase of players blessing themselves as they emerge from the dressing rooms or making the sign of the cross in thanksgiving when a goal is scored. Recently, Linvoy Stephen Primus crossed my path when he came to the local school to raise funds for a third-world charity. As I listened to this man, I realised that he is a remarkable missionary for Christ and a great ambassador for Christianity.

He speaks in layman's terms about his faith in Jesus. With a profound conviction, he uses the language of a good steward in that he claims that his football skills are given to him by God. In playing well he is giving the talent back to God. Good football is giving God the glory.

He claims that miracles have taken place in his life. He was brought up as a Christian, with parents from a strong Caribbean background. But in those days, he claims that Sunday school and Church were a cold experience. He has now gone full circle and has become an inspirational role model for many aspiring young people. He does inspiring work in many schools along the South Coast.

When a major national daily paper headlines a footballer as a 'miracle man' but not for his football skills one should sit up to take notice. This was how *The Times* recently described Fabrice Muamba.

When he collapsed with a massive cardiac arrest at White Hart Lane in front of a live television audience, the people of the nation went into overdrive with prayer. Although he was presumed dead, he came back to life.

Amazing things began to happen; an unknown African cleaner came into Fabrice's intensive care unit each day to pray in the corner; on another occasion, he woke up to hear the Pope calling on everybody to pray for Muamba. It turned out to be Archbishop Nichols. Within hours of him landing in hospital, people across the nation wore printed jerseys - 'Pray for Muamba'.

Not since Diana was the whole nation caught up in prayer and this for a young footballer whose heart had stopped for 76 minutes. This man too has inspired the nation by his own personal prayer and his humility. Subsequently, he claims that he owes his life to a miracle as a result of the prayer.

But the greatest accolade must go to Didier Drogba. In 2007 the United Nation Development Programme appointed him a goodwill ambassador. He was born in the Ivory Coast and there his heart lies.

He plays international football for his country. It

is through football that he has an utter conviction that he can achieve reconciliation between the warring factions in his homeland. He has established a foundation to build a much needed £3 million hospital in Abidjan. He could easily become the president of his country.

There is a new missionary spirit at work in some of our footballers. It is evangelisation in reverse. With the colonies, Christians from Europe took the Good News all over the world with miraculous results. They brought a sense of justice, a healthy desire for freedom but most of all the love of Jesus Christ in abundance.

My mother was a great devotee of 'a penny' for the 'black babies'. She would be astonished at how the contents of those little collection boxes have come back to bless western culture. Of course, the missionary spirit in reverse is not just confined to footballers. In the Diocese of Portsmouth, we have three priests from Bamenda, Cameroon. With a wonderful visionary spirit, Bishop Derek Worlock established strong links with West Africa by sending priests when we had plenty. Now it is our turn to be the recipients of missionary endeavours. Like my mother, Derek would be astonished at how things turned out.

These are only a few of the highly paid footballers who are wonderful ambassadors for Christ. Apparently, there are over 65 Christian footballers in the English and Scottish Leagues. It also appears that more and more are declaring their faith, not just as Christians, but as Jews and Muslims too. There is a profound lesson for the Churches to learn from all sports personalities with faith. While we have no problem with football having borrowed many of our treasured rituals, we need to rediscover how they can retain their fan base even when they are losing or are relegated.

Christianity has many believers, but we have lost a sense of belonging to a worldwide club that we take pride in. Alienation can be caused by a community that has lost its way in trying to preserve an old-fashioned structure that simply does not fit into a 21st century culture. A real sense of belonging to the fan club is a profound deficit in modern Christianity. I know several people who would be adamant that they are Catholics, but we see them at Mass on Christmas Day and Easter, if we are lucky. You would be termed a poor football supporter if you only went to one match every season.

(Citation: GRUFFERTY, T. December 2012. *The Tablet*)

Pilgrimages

The next session is dedicated to Pilgrimages. I have done some wonderful journeys with other people, mostly with parishioners, but also pilgrimages on my own. This is a wonderful ministry with prayer, reflection, inspiration, and real humour. It is amazing to see how people are transformed once they step into a new landscape. It is also interesting to observe the very tiny minority who clearly point out that they will not be changed by this journey. In at least two cases they returned home with a completely different mentality and a hugely different spiritual place. You can see this also in pilgrimages filmed for TV in recent years.

How to be a Pilgrim

- Never complain or moan.
- Always PRAISE.
- The best thing about your destination is not the food, nor the weather, but the people.
- The people you meet are always the happiest people, because you are happy.
- Give something back, especially if you have been enriched yourself.
- Forget your mobile or iPad
- Before you visit a historic place, do your own research and share it with others, if the opportunity arises.
- The best pilgrim sights are not on your mobile but before your eyes.
- Always remember that you can hear, feel, and touch Holy Ground.
- Eat or drink something that you would never do at home.
- You might be in a Hotel but remember that your fellow guests are also Pilgrims.

- ❖ Try to listen to the Guide and only rarely repeat what he/she says.
- ❖ Always say "thank you".
- ❖ Return home with at least five new words you never used before.
- ❖ Avoid buying local rubbish and only think about shopping once a day.
- ❖ Congratulate your fellow Pilgrims on their energy and enthusiasm.
- ❖ Never take a selfie. If you want a photo of yourself, ask a fellow pilgrim or, better still, a local to take a photo of you, but always with other people and with a Pilgrimage site as a backdrop.

God is speaking:

Good Morning Pilgrim.

I am the God of Israel. Today I will be handling all your affairs.

If you come across a situation you cannot handle, do not attempt to resolve it yourself.

Just place it in SFJTD (something for Jesus to do) box. It will be addressed IN MY TIME NOT YOURS.

Once the matter has been placed in the box, do not hold on to it or change it or remove it. Holding on or removal might well delay resolution of your problem. Because I do not sleep nor slumber, there is no need for you to lose any sleep. Rest my child. If you need to contact me, I am only a prayer away.

Love you lots. The Lord God of history out.

Almighty Father Look down upon these humble Pilgrims.

A Pilgrim Prayer

We are doomed to walk this way, taking photos, selfies and shopping.

Guide us to the best sights and the best places to eat where the food is superb.

Give us the strength to see everything and follow our leader.

Prevent us from wishing to 'go native' in wanting a nap in the afternoon.

Help all women in the group from buying bargains not needed.

And be merciful to all men who complain about everything.

Make us all punctual and ready for every surprise.

Amen

Pilgrimage to the Holy Land - Year of Faith 2013

The Year of Faith is a propitious occasion for people to understand more profoundly that the foundation of our Christian faith is an encounter with Christ – an encounter that can help us rediscover our faith, according to Pope Emeritus Benedict XVI. One of his pastoral recommendations for this year was to encourage pilgrimages.

As part of our parish programme during this Year of Faith, I organised a group of parishioners and their friends from southeast Hampshire (mainly Catholics with a few Anglicans, including a church warden) to travel to the Holy Land, the place which first saw the presence of Christ. The programme was designed to help people encounter Christ by walking in his footsteps. And, when a parish group makes a pilgrimage like this, the time spent together as they share the experience in common helps them to notice where they encounter him in their everyday lives.

Our first day was dedicated to a prayerful walk through the Old Walled City of Jerusalem. An early morning call to prayer came from the minaret of the mosque across from the Ecce Homo Hospice on the Via Dolorosa, where we were staying. Our walk began there as we followed the path Jesus took on his way to the Cross. At the ancient Church of the Holy Sepulchre, all the bells were bellowing a cacophony of sound out across the city, as if to welcome us.

The Holy Sepulchre is shared by six different Christian occupants – Latin Catholics, Greek Orthodox, Armenian Orthodox, Syrians, Copts, and Ethiopians – each suspiciously watching the others for any infringement of rights on this holiest piece of real estate.

We are the same body of Christ; but different parts

make up the whole jigsaw – each wanting to pray in the place where Jesus died and rose from the dead.

Jerusalem itself is a mighty mishmash as you observe devout Jews rushing to wail at the Western Wall, Muslims going in the same direction to pray in the Dome of the Rock, while Christians gather around a simple cross on the way up to Mount Calvary. The international blend of peoples, smells and sounds adds to the rich fabric of one of the greatest cities in the world.

From Jerusalem, the view to the east is blocked by the Mount of Olives, which is about 100 metres above the city. The road runs along the top of the ridge, and the views over the Old City are magnificent. Jesus was familiar with this place; when He was in Jerusalem, He stayed with friends at Bethany (Luke 10:38; Mark 11:11).

As pilgrims sit on the slope opposite the Temple Mount, they can reflect on what it must have been like when Jesus sat here speaking to His disciples of the future of the city (Mark 13:3) whose lack of faith had driven Him to tears (Luke 19:37, 41-44). Some may even identify with Jesus when they think about how many in their parishes are lacking in faith.

Walking down the Mount of Olives, the pilgrim finds Dominus Flevit, the church in the shape of a tear, commemorating that occasion when Jesus wept. At the bottom of the slope is the Garden of Gethsemane, where Jesus went after the Passover meal. He told the disciples He was grieved and asked them to stay awake while He prayed. He asked them to pray that they would not fall into temptation; but, when He returned, they were asleep.

Like us, Jesus knew the disciples were the ones who were in danger of resisting the will of God by resisting Jesus' imminent death on the Cross.

He also knew the disillusioned disciples would scatter when he was arrested, and when it became clear that they had been wrong about how and when the

Kingdom would come about.

As we prayed in the garden for all those we know who are in agony, we prayed too that our parishes would be places where they would find people attentive to them – places where people are helped to be open to the will of God.

Any pilgrimage to the Holy Land must include a visit to Bethlehem. Joseph and Mary had to go to Bethlehem, a journey that presented them with problems; gaining access to the town today still presents difficulties. The chaos of the place of the Nativity contrasts with the tranquillity of the Catholic church just a few feet away. Here, one easily finds the time to ponder the significance of the Incarnation. One can also ponder the issues facing those seeking political asylum and the many people the world over who have nowhere to live – and to ask what our parishes are doing to help them.

Our pilgrimage continued with Jesus beckoning us on to reflect on His Galilean ministry. Celebrating Mass on Sunday morning by the shores of the Sea of Galilee and hearing the Gospel on a boat with the engine silent, allows the power of the Word to settle deep within the inner person. All around Galilee, the stories, the miracles, and the sayings of Jesus come alive. This is especially true when you read the Sermon on the Mount in the Church of the Beatitudes high above the lake, echoing each of the beatitudes so that they resound within each of us.

In Cana, married couples were invited to renew their vows – and those who were not married were invited to pray for them and to reflect on different ways they can support married couples in their parishes. We live in times in which marriage needs direct affirmation in parish life. Everyone was invited to renew their baptismal promises in the River Jordan, at the place where it is likely Jesus was baptised – a very powerful experience.

Modern Nazareth is dominated by the massive

Basilica of the Annunciation, built to enclose and protect the discoveries made during an exhaustive archaeological excavation. The apse belonged to a small, 18-metre-long church of the mid-fifth century, itself built over what might have been a synagogue where Jesus could easily have declared the Lord's Year of Favour. We prayed that the Year of Faith will be a year of favour. To journey with Jesus in His homeland is one way to come to know him more deeply – and pilgrims return home to share that experience with others. It is an experience I would encourage every parish to consider.

(Citation: GRUFFERTY, T. August 2013. *The Tablet*)

Southampton - Pilgrim Fathers & Mothers

Being stood up is sometimes not an accident and can be beneficial. I had a lunch appointment recently with a friend in the centre of Southampton, but they never showed. I went for a walk around the City Walls only to make some amazing discoveries. I found the Mayflower Monument to the Pilgrim Fathers, who left the city in two ships, the Mayflower, and the Speedwell in July1620. After a hazardous journey to the New World, only the Mayflower landed in Cape Cod in November the same year. Many of the passengers and half the crew had died. Near the Mayflower monument is a lonely looking pub called 'Titanic' as a reminder of another fatal transatlantic crossing 300 years later.

My spirits were lifted with a visit to the delightful St Joseph's Catholic Church in Bugle Street. Here is a peaceful haven for prayer and reflection in an otherwise busy city.

The building is rich in history. As the Mother Church of Catholics in the City, it can easily be described as 'A Little Gem'. During the French Revolution, devout Catholics including priests arrived in Southampton in great numbers. In October 1796, there were forty French priests in Southampton. It is recorded that they received a subsistence allowance of £67.10.2 per month. It took another 30 years before firm foundations were laid for a presbytery and a church. A Fr Watkins enters the history of Southampton. He acquired a large Georgian House in St Michael's Square with a large garden running parallel with Bugle Street. He had plans to build a chapel in the garden. The new church was officially dedicated with 18 priests on 30th October 1830. It was the first Catholic Church in the country dedicated to St Joseph since the Reformation.

It may interest you to know that the same Fr

Watkins subsequently went on a great adventure to Sydney and Adelaide travelling around the Cape of Good Hope. Nothing else is heard of him until it is recorded in a school log of his hometown Abergavenny, 'School closed today for the funeral of Fr Watkins. All children attended'.

You will need to stand in St Michael's Square facing the Anglican Church with the same name to soak up history. Also examine the architecture and the symmetry of the whole square. You can easily imagine being in Tudor England. Also ponder all those people 'going down to the Sea in ships'. The Pilgrim Fathers and Mothers were brave souls.

If you want to do the tour with an official guide, there is a tour every Sunday at 11.30 a.m. leaving from 2 Lions at Bar Gate but check with Tourist Information, St Joseph, Bugle Street, Southampton SG142AH
http://www.discoversouthampton.co.uk/visit

(Citation: GRUFFERTY, T. July 2016. *Portsmouth People*)

A Pilgrimage to Reading, Berkshire June 2010.

Somebody reminded me recently that not everyone can go on Pilgrimage to Jerusalem, Rome or Lourdes. The remark prompted me to think about special places of Prayer nearer home.

Our Lady of Caversham was the first place to come to mind. The shrine dates to at least 1106 and was located near St. Peter's Church. There were strong associations with Caversham Bridge crossing the River Thames. There is a famous holy well and its waters had healing qualities. Famous visitors included Queen Catherine of Aragon on 17th July 1532. Far from me to suggest anything, but the shrine itself was destroyed six years after the famous Queen's visit!

Apparently the well still survives and can be found at the top of Priest Hill. With the building of the new Catholic Church of Our Lady and St. Anne in the 1880's, the Shrine of Our Lady of Caversham was revived and is worth a visit. Contact the Parish Priest, The Presbytery, 2 South View Avenue, Caversham, Reading, RG4 5AB. Tel: 0118 947 1787 Email: **stanne@frmartin.plus.com**

Across the river and in our Diocese is Reading Abbey Ruins. The Abbey was a later foundation to the Caversham Shrine, but it became a more famous place of pilgrimage in Medieval England. The Abbey had numerous royal visitors, most especially Henry III, who stayed several weeks four times a year. There could be an increasing interest in the Abbey Ruins if the tomb of Henry I is found under a car park as seems likely. The story of Richard III in Leicester could happen on our doorstep! Where will the reburial take place?

Reading Abbey contained many royal treasures, including 230 relics, one of which was the hand of St. James. There was a strong association with Santiago de

Compostela. The Abbey was recognised as an official stop on the Camino. The ancient pilgrims followed 'The Pilgrim Way' to the coast and crossed the Channel at Southampton and Portsmouth.

As at Caversham, the Abbey was destroyed in 1538 with **Blessed Hugh Farrington** being the last Abbot. He was charged and found guilty of high treason and executed in 1539. He is patron of the Catholic secondary school in the town. There are well preserved ruins which are worth exploration, including a fine Arch Way and an interior Chapter House. Make sure you visit St. James Catholic Church built within the Abbey Grounds. Contact the Parish Priest who will give you a warm welcome. **www.jameswilliam-reading.org.uk** **(Citation: GRUFFERTY, T. September 2010.***Portsmouth People***)**

Pilgrimage to Canterbury – May 2009

This Pilgrimage follows on, because for centuries pilgrims followed the South Downs Way from Winchester, the ancient capital of England to Canterbury. In my journey, during my recent sabbatical, far from the famous route, I used a modern means of transport with a sat-nav to reach the famous UNESCO heritage city of Thomas à Becket. I had the great privilege to meander around Canterbury for a few days. Almost immediately, I established a strong identity with the people who have been around the town since 597 when St. Augustine baptised the Saxon King Ethelbert.

For historical reasons, Canterbury is quite different to any other place of pilgrimage I know. That may well be due to the dramatic decline of pilgrims since Tudor days. There are signs that the pilgrims are back in great numbers, perhaps only outnumbered by tourists from the Continent. I am 100% certain that all tourists are enchanted by the spiritual riches of the Cathedral precincts.

A pilgrim to Canterbury is in contact with Thomas à Becket who was murdered in the ancient building a few days after Christmas in 1170. The visit to the place where his tomb and relics once were recalls the beautiful sermon T. S. Eliot included in his play about Becket entitled: 'Murder in the Cathedral'.

One also meets fellow pilgrims immortalised by Geoffrey Chaucer in the 'Canterbury Tales'. These are the same today as ever. The arrogant merchant walks side by side with the faithless preachers, the holy nun in her vow of silence walks with those silent ones who never tell a tale. These characters are as alive today as in the 14th century.

T. S. and Geoffrey had a profound sense of the inner sanctum of the human being in tune with the inner holiness of places like Canterbury Cathedral. Before you go, make sure you catch up with an excellent three-part documentary on BBC 2. (Use iPlayer).

The tiny Catholic Church of St. Thomas of Canterbury, within spitting distance of its mighty neighbour, is a great delight made more special by Eucharistic Adoration. Make sure you visit after you leave the Cathedral.

Pilgrimage to Florence – Summer 2012

As I inter-railed around Italy, Florence was one of my biggest attractions. Since I used 'Monastery Stays' as an introduction to accommodation, I found myself in a convent in the heart of Florence. The sister in charge of guests is an animated religious with a great enthusiasm for looking after her visitors. She had just been given a hi-tech language translator which resulted in hoots of laughter throughout the corridors of the semi-silent ancient residence. I think I was the first person she used this gadget on. The machine was not able to cope with spoken English with an Irish accent. By the time I left, the machine had a serious nervous breakdown but not without loud knots of laughter from the nuns' common room.

Florence holds many other outstanding attractions. It has symbols of the Medici family on every street and on every monument. In Florence you meet Dante, Leonardo de Vinci, Machiavelli, Botticelli, Michelangelo, and Donatello, not to mention my favourite artist Caravaggio who lived in the city before he became famous.

Florence is dripping with Renaissance art. The finest pieces are found in the Uffizi Gallery. I discovered the best time to visit is just after 5 pm when all day trippers have returned to their hotels or the cruise ships. This is the best place in the world for religious art and if you just allow it to touch your inner self, you can grow very tall spiritually in minutes. The piece that inspires me most is Michelangelo's 'Nativity'. The bare feet of Mary and Joseph on green grass speaks volumes about the birth of Jesus being real and earthy. Walk out of the Gallery and immediately you see the Duomo which dominates the city and the surrounding Tuscan countryside.

If you want a stunning insight into the Cathedral, I recommend you watch 'Invisible Italy-Florence' with Alexander Armstrong and Michael Scott. Catch up with

BBC iPlayer. Even with 3D scanning technology, I am not sure they solve how Brunelleschi capped the famous dome. The Cathedral and the surrounds make a celebrated statement about our glorious past, about the wonderful present and about a bright future. If humans can achieve such wonders, we hold the divine within and without. To ponder beauty combined with symmetry is a profound prayer with the eyes of the soul. That is the goal of all pilgrimage.

This time I fell in love with the Ponte Vecchio for the simple reason that thousands of young romantics have sealed their love with locks to the railings on the ancient bridge.

When in Florence, make sure you do a day trip to its great rival, Pisa and if there, you may as well visit Lucca. Another must see place is Siena where the presence of the powerful Catherine still pervades the streets of this lovely city.

A Private Pilgrimage to Rome to see St. Matthew.

In my tour around Italy last year, the goal of my pilgrimage was Rome. I emphasise that I was a pilgrim, not a tourist. A pilgrimage to Rome should always include one or two specific things to do and see. There is so much to experience in Rome that, unless you target a few things, you can leave with serious spiritual indigestion, or even something more terminal.

On this trip, I focused on Michelangelo from the town of Caravaggio. I was especially interested in his painting of 'The Calling of Matthew' in the Church of St. Louis of France. I really wanted to reflect on Matthew because his year in the Lectionary was approaching. I was not disappointed, as instantly you see the only tax collector Evangelist and the only Apostle in that profession called by Jesus with the point of a finger.

Matthew's reaction is twofold- he keeps his hand firmly on the money on the table, like any good tax collector, but, more importantly, he looks totally in disbelief that anyone should call him into anything different, most of all Jesus. How many people do you know who are called by a finger?

The Church of St. Louis has another treasure of Caravaggio, 'The Martyrdom of St. Matthew'. The artist produced both paintings around the same time. He was not without his personal problems that are frequently reflected in his works. In his confusion, he went from one to the other only to be inspired again and again. His personal darkness is reflected especially in the 'Martyrdom' but notice how Matthew the Saint emerges from the hostility and darkness around him.

That light and darkness are also clearly visible in another famous Caravaggio that was on display in the National Gallery London last year, 'The Taking of Jesus'.

I love the second story of this painting because it was missing and not recognised for over 200 years. It was owned by William Hamilton Nisbet and hung in his house in Scotland until 1921. Later he sold it to an Irish woman, Marie Lea-Wilson who eventually gave it to the Jesuits in Dublin.

It hung, unrecognised, in their dining room, until 1990. Then Father Noel Barber SJ asked the Senior Conservator of the National Gallery to examine the painting with the view to cleaning and restoring it. When the cleaning process began it slowly dawned on the experts who the original genius was. The wonder of an outstanding Baroque pioneer!

The painting is now on permanent loan to the National Gallery of Ireland. The most prominent aspect of being a pilgrim, rather than a tourist, is when you aim to be in Rome, you actually finish up in Dublin.

(Citation: GRUFFERTY, T. November 2009. *Portsmouth People*)

Pilgrimage to Milan

In September 2016, I spent some fascinating days inter-railing around north and central Italy, re-visiting places I had been before and discovering new ones. I make no apology for using the excellent Italian train system for my pilgrimage. I started off in Milan where you might be surprised to find many hallowed places. I had three in mind: -

The Duomo must be one of the most majestic Gothic churches in the world. The 135 spires are startling, with their numerous statues and gargoyles. Despite very strict armed security, you can still climb on to the roof, from where you get a magnificent view of the Alps to the North. You can easily spend hours in the Square admiring the front of the building. My attention was caught by a huge TV screen immediately to the left of the building advertising Samsung - the sacred and the profane brought together with the ancient and the modern.

There is plenty of modernity in Milan, especially in fashion for men and women. It was strange to see men wearing warm coats, scarves, and hats in 23 degrees of September sunshine!

My second hallowed place was the refectory of Santa Maria delle Grazie, where I went to view Leonardo da Vinci's 'Last Supper'. Gaining entry is fraught with difficulties, and at first, you wonder why there is all the fuss. Standing immediately in front of the masterpiece, one can feel a deep disappointment because it has almost faded away. Hardly visible is the depiction of the moment when Jesus points out: 'one of you will betray me' (Matt 26:21).

An enhanced image of Leonardo da Vinci's 'Last Supper' featured in *Singulart Magazine* 14/04/2019. Da Vinci's original work dates from 1495-1498.

Da Vinci wanted to capture the reactions of the disciples to those words of Jesus. The reactions range from shock, surprise, anger, and upset to incredulity. When seen at close quarters, the painting contains many surprises. For example, there is the use of three: three windows; the apostles seated in groups of three; and the figure of Jesus forming a triangle. Many enthusiasts have explored the significance of three in the mind of the genius and most conclude that Leonardo had the Trinity in mind.

However, the real surprise and shock comes when you step backwards from the masterpiece. We were told to walk backwards and keep our eyes fixed firmly on the painting. I cannot tell you what happens because it would be like revealing the secret of an outstanding story. For you to know now before you have seen the work would be a personal betrayal on my part. You must see this masterpiece for yourself. When you do, watch out for the finale. It is as good as it gets.

Having spent four days absorbed in the architecture of ancient and modern Milan, I then caught a terribly slow train to Lake Maggiore. The Lake has several places well worth visiting, but I opted for the main resort called Stresa. A cable car there whisks you to the top of Monte Mottarone from where there are spectacular views of the surrounding mountains. The fact that this is Charles Borromeo's territory gives an added dimension to a very spiritual delight. Every inch of the lakes of Northern Italy, with the surrounding mountains, is Holy Ground.

> *'I lift up my eyes to the mountains-- where does my help come from?' (Psalm 121).*

(Citation: GRUFFERTY, T. January *Portsmouth People*)

Pilgrimage to Croagh Patrick

Reek Sunday, Last Sunday of July –
Croagh Patrick, Co. Mayo

Reek Sunday is an especially important tradition in the West of Ireland. As many as ten thousand people climb the holy mountain of Croagh Patrick in Co. Mayo on the last Sunday of July. These days, many people climb the Reek throughout the year. There is a chapel at the top of the mountain where Mass is celebrated every hour during the Sunday morning. This year, I decided to carry out a little survey at the statue of St. Patrick on Reek Sunday.

I was particularly interested in what young people thought and I asked the question: 'Was climbing Croagh Patrick a spiritual experience?' I asked the question out of a conviction that if young people have stopped going to Mass, the Church needs to discover what engages them spiritually. Many people these days respond to real needs and receive blessings galore from responding to those needs. Therein they find a spirituality at a deep level.

I think we should be constantly reviewing why people stop going to Mass, but also be open to discovering where and how they find fulfilment. We should do so with a critical analysis of where the Church is going wrong. Before I started, I counted 100 adults coming down the mountain and 65 of them were under 30.

Here are some of the replies from those young people I spoke to:

'I was completely transformed; my view of Mayo was completely transformed. It was an experience full of personal reflection, prayer and contemplation'.

'I got great satisfaction especially when I reached the summit. It was a real therapy for me'.

'I really got to know my three friends and all of us have promised to do it every year'.

'It is the most inspiring thing we have done since we got married seven years ago. We are going to have a lovely meal in Westport'.

A young father of three children (aged between 7-12) said it was a bonding experience for all five members of the family.

'I prayed, went to confession and attended Mass in the Little Church at the summit, but nothing has changed today'.

'I saw the whole of my life in miniature because when I wanted to stop and turn back, every new step upwards towards the summit was a new victory'.

'I never set foot in any church before, but I did enter the Chapel at the summit. This was a new experience as I felt at peace'.

Many said they were there because a family member did the climb 30 years ago and they now felt they should do the same.

One person from America said nothing had changed. But he used the word 'serene' at least five times.

Several people said they did the Reek because a family member was not well.

Many young people did not understand what 'a spiritual experience' was but more females felt better about the challenge than males.

Young families were very evident.

The conditions for this Reek Sunday were ideal. At least two people used the word 'therapy', which fascinated me because that is more a medical word than a religious word.

I was really enriched myself with the interaction with people. If people have given up the Church, I am convinced, we need to dialogue with them so that we can provide other options.

Just because people have stopped going to Mass

does not mean they have lost their spiritual dynamism or their idealism. Many people do the annual climb without any religious conviction or Church affiliation.

'Whoever claims to abide in Jesus, ought to walk as he walked' (1 John 2:3-11).

A Pilgrimage along the Wild Atlantic Way

When you think about Pilgrimage, we usually consider other people on the journey with us from the point of departure to the destination? Our fellow pilgrims are sometimes challenging, and frequently unpredictable. That makes for a fascinating journey and throws up extraordinary surprises.

Because I am currently on sabbatical, I decided to do a solitary pilgrimage. I looked around for aids to help me on my journey. I struggled for a long time until I happened on a very special calendar for 2018 called *Relax with Art*. With the calendar came loads of different coloured pencils. I opted to spend 30 minutes each day without all the daily sounds, especially the radio.

Here are some of the positive results. It is amazing how 30 minutes of focus can lighten the daily routine. Using different colours on the page opens up new colours in nature even in midwinter.

Because I was living in Co. Mayo I was automatically drawn in my mind to the Wild Atlantic Way. This is the longest defined coastal route in the world stretching from North Donegal to Kinsale in West Cork. This is really at the edge of Europe and at every stage you could easily let your spirits roam free as you put the finishing touches to the green colours on the calendar. There is no room for Blues in this part of the solitary pilgrimage. The best pilgrimages always include wildness about them, and the Wild Atlantic Way does not disappoint.

You also begin to see the colour of other people and, in the most surprising ways, you begin to do an audit of your own personal journey. The audit often continues for hours in a gentle way. In the olden days we called it 'the examination of conscience'. You discover that with meditation there comes mindfulness. The 30 minutes of silence helps you to listen to every sound with greater care. You look at everything with a different focus and immediately you see the harmony of everything around you.

But such a pilgrimage as this also highlights the incongruity of things from fashion to architecture, and the difference between lakes and mountains. When was the last time you noticed the conflict of colours on the sanctuary of your parish church? Pope Francis invites us to lift up our hearts, our minds to see what is around us in order to see the harmony and the tranquillity of nature.

With my colouring calendar I was drawn to Ballintubber Abbey to find an ancient sense of harmony and, dare I say, to find beauty in ancient architecture. I did some of my colouring inside the Abbey Church. Mass has been celebrated here consistently since 1216. This became my most prayerful and reflective session in recent years. Long before 1216 the little village had had strong folklore links with Saint Patrick, who is reputed to have walked from Ballintubber to Croagh Patrick where he fasted for 40 days and nights. Wonderful work has been carried out in the Abbey Church and in the grounds by the current Parish Priest, Fr. Frank Fahy, including a modern Stations of the Cross, a Rosary Way and an underground permanent Crib.

On the last Sunday of July, Croagh Patrick attracts thousands of pilgrims, some of whom climb the mountain in bare feet. The panoramic views across Clew Bay feature beautifully in the Wild Atlantic Way. On a clear day the views are awe-inspiring. So much so that there is no time and no reason to have your head in colouring-in a calendar. The views across the Bay give you a real sense of wellbeing. You are indeed blessed if a simple colouring book can lead you to such heights- even in the mind!

There are as many pilgrimages as there are people

because your journey is different from mine and it's a great blessing even with a simple colouring book if you discover that we are on an epic pilgrimage of life itself.
(Citation: GRUFFERTY, T. January 2018. *Portsmouth People***)**

Pilgrimage to Lough Derg...
A Wholly Detox

As I drove north out of Sligo Town on the N15, I was prompted several times to spend a few lovely days around Killybegs. After all I was on holiday. My green VW Polo instinctively turned right following a sign for Pettigo and Lough Derg. Almost immediately the landscape changed dramatically as I encountered a barren if beautiful countryside. The entrance to St Patrick's Purgatory on the island of Lough Derg takes you by surprise.

There still a little time to turn the car round and head for the fleshpots of Donegal. But it is quite easy to get on to the island. You pay your 45 Euro and you are given clear instructions on how to get the boat across. The boat whisks you across the choppy waters to the penitential island in a truly short time. By now, you have digested your instructions which are direct and simple. You are allocated a bunk bed with the number and invited to leave your belongings on the bed. But most important of all, to remove your shoes and your socks for the duration of your stay.

The removal of shoes has a deeper impact on the pilgrim then it first appears. In fact, a barefooted pilgrim is one in common with everybody else on the island. This common denominator has profound implications for all those taking part. Regardless of your position on the mainland, you immediately realise that there is in the human psyche, a vulnerability and poverty in common with your fellow pilgrims. If death is a great leveller, then taking off your shoes on holy ground has a similar affect.

The bare feet affect every minute of your stay on the island. The bare feet draw you almost immediately into a desire for change and therefore penance, especially a walk around the penitential beds. These are dedicated to various Saints. Some are more difficult than others. It is rumoured that a member of the island staff sharpens the stones at the beginning of the season every year. A woman on the boat told me this was her 27th time doing Lough Derg and the beds were getting harder year by year. She looked rather puzzled when I said that I preferred a soft bed.

There are serious exercises which take you into the night and into the next morning. The first night you are expected to be fully awake for the entire duration. But the exercises also lead you deeper still. These is a well-planned routine which keeps you fully awake until 10.00 p.m. on the second night of your stay. By now you have got to know your fellow pilgrims and there were 125 plus. There are various psychological barriers, especially during darkness, which have to be conquered if the program is to succeed, and it is amazing how helpful your companions are in gatecrashing those obstacles.

Some excellent liturgies also help you to overcome these barriers. Our two evening Masses were thought-provoking, challenging and very prayerful. The excellent music, good preaching and a wonderful involvement of laypeople were all inspirational. There is also the spiritual sustenance drawn from reflecting on the stained-glass windows of Harry Clarke, the most famous stained-glass genius of the last century. What happens at a deep personal level is truly profound. For every single person, the experience is different and all the more beautiful. It is equally different every time you go, and that is why people do the pilgrimage frequently.

In Lough Derg, you are confronted with the person you are. The first thing that hits you between the eyes is your own personal weaknesses, but this is quickly followed by your strengths, and the spiritual powers, of course, win out in the end. Regardless of your faith, even if you have no faith at all, you are challenged to face the inner person.

This is the greatest personal detox on the face of the earth. At excellent rates, you have the best clean out for your body, mind, soul, and spirit. This is better than any known medication or therapist.

The exercise in the prayer, private and communal, fasting and the deprivation of sleep draw together every fibre of the person in a great battle between body and soul. I am delighted to say that the spiritual always wins for those who wholeheartedly enter the wilderness of the island.

In truth, there is no other option because the usual things we rely on are not allowed on the holy place, mobile phones, laptops, iPads and cameras. Because of this, you are naked of the things we have come to rely on, and the removal of the shoes enables the radical change. In a very clever way, you are brought low that you might reach the skies. You go down to the depths that you might reach the stars. In the image of another great Pilgrim you are buried in the grave that you might experience the Resurrection.

Dare I say this - on Saint Patrick's holy island there is a great mixture of Pagan, Celtic and Christian spirituality blended to draw the best out of the participating pilgrim. It is essential to do Lough Derg at least every 10 years. This is the best value B&B in the world, except of course there is no breakfast. I have not mentioned fasting which is an important a feature of your stay on the island. There is, of course, a great compensation for all your efforts, namely a wonderful night's sleep for the pure, the innocent and the radically different person who will return to the fleshpots of the mainland in the morning!

(Citation: GRUFFERTY, T. November 2006.
Intercom Magazine)

Pilgrimage to Malta

Caravaggio's 'St Jerome, writing' (1607-1608)

There are as many pilgrimages as there are people apart from Ireland and the UK, Malta must be one of the most outstanding islands in the world. Its people have a powerful faith built on the foundations of Acts 28:1-10. Before you go any further, read the passage, if for no other reason than St Luke himself might well be also be linked to the Maltese people. You cannot have any better connections to the New Testament than to have associations with Paul, the greatest evangeliser, and Luke the evangelist. As the writer of the fifth Gospel (Acts), Luke himself may well have been shipwrecked in St Paul's Bay.

Even without Luke, the Maltese have lived, thrived, and survived on St. Paul's generous compliment to them in the New Testament. It is Paul's greatest tribute to any race and the tribute continues with great strength, based on my recent experience. I have visited the Island several times over the years but, for some strange reason, I have missed out on another famous visitor, Caravaggio. He too experienced a shipwreck in another sense and, happily for Malta, he leaves behind two outstanding works of art.

These days we talk about enlightened techno art on social media, but Caravaggio was ahead of the revolution of light with an enlightened mind. I stood spellbound for a very long time before St Jerome with his naked torso shining against the cardinal's hat.

Out of curiosity, I asked six fellow visitors about the red hat, but none saw it. Everybody saw the Word being translated by Jerome. With his powerful use of light, Caravaggio was himself an Evangelist and I would not be at all surprised if this was his intention. We now get three famous Evangelists on one small island- an itinerant preacher, a medical doctor who writes beautifully, and a troubled soul who paints with vision, imagination and with extraordinary power.

The other great painting in Valletta is the 'Beheading of John the Baptist'. This is the only piece of art which Caravaggio signed, and the signature is shown in the blood spilling from throat of the slain Baptiser. Why? Like so many other gifted people, Michelangelo from the village of Caravaggio never did anything without a purpose. So, you can guess the reason, dear reader, and I will leave you to reason it out.

Both works are housed in a most exquisite setting beside the Cathedral. I cannot finish this piece on Malta without clearly pointing out that, if you want to get in contact with Paul, simply contact the Maltese people as he is in their blood, their DNA, in every parade of shops and even in their national emblems.

(Citation: GRUFFERTY, T. January 2018. *Portsmouth People***)**

August 21st Apparition Day Knock – The Praying Crows of Knock Shrine

There is nothing I love more than to sit outside the Apparition Chapel in Knock on a warm summer evening. The pilgrims are gone, the traffic on the road close-by is almost non-existent, there are a few people in the Apparition Chapel attending Eucharistic Adoration. Usually, I am alone in the warm sunshine as it beams in from the West.

Here is a perfect setting on which to meditate on those who appeared on the gable of the old church on August 21, 1879. I try to do this at roughly the time that Mrs. Campbell, Margaret Byrne and the other witnesses saw the heavenly figures on that Thursday evening 140 years ago. I have learned in recent years the prayer of Mindfulness which helps focus on Mary with her eyes looking up to heaven in prayer.

I have a great love for St. Joseph, as I seem to have stalked him in the three parishes that I have worked in. The last person I become mindful of is St. John, and I usually have his Gospel with me. Of all three heavenly visitors, John is the only one who has eye contact with the visionaries and with us. I invite him especially to speak directly to me and he never fails to do so with eloquence. 'I am the light of the world' (John 8:12) is very profound as the shadows of the evening gather. 'The truth will set you free' (John 8:32)) is often a counterbalance to the events at the ending of the day.

The greatest evening prayer for me must be: 'From his fullness we have received favour upon favour' (John 1:16). As Knock is nearly always breezy, the wind plays a crucial part of the Pilgrimage. You hear it, you feel it, but you don't know where it comes from or where it goes.

It is exactly like that with the Holy Spirit. At this stage in my prayer Mary usually interjects with 'They have no wine' (John 2:3). The response from her son at the festival described in John 7:37 is always the same: 'Let anyone who is thirsty come to me and those who believe, drink'.

I always read Chapter 10 of St. John because it leads me to the Lamb in the Cable Chapel. The Lamb invites me to walk through the gateway where I will find food and, walk in and out freely. The Lamb knows me and gives me eternal life. At this stage in my mindfulness there is a major interruption when the silence of the evening is scattered. The wildlife of Mayo takes over with gusto. Any thought of any further prayer is placed on the back burner. All the crows of Connaught suddenly swarm like a giant tsunami from nowhere. They fly over the Parish Church, usually in clockwise direction and most of them do so three times.

Pilgrims usually walk around the Church praying the Rosary in anti-clockwise fashion, but the crows make their own prayerful statement. Having done their ritual, they then fly en masse to the Basilica. Some fly straight to the upper storey and form a straight line, while others perch themselves on lower levels.

Many of the birds face towards the old Parish Church, the Apparition Chapel, and the warm evening sunshine. With the white facade of the Basilica, the black feathers of the crows add a picturesque addition to the building. Most of the birds stay still for a long time, while others play with each other in a romantic fashion. I wonder if they are teenage crows! Others still fly around squawking as if they are calling others to join them. That call for unity and fellowship can last for some time. Eventually, all are gathered in and they depart in unison for the night.

I have observed this phenomenon frequently so much so that the birds of the air have become part of my prayer. It is not without some irony that Isaiah says those with faith will soar on wings like eagles (Isaiah 40:31). On one occasion, I rushed home to research the spiritual significance of the crow, only to find that crows like to be around people, which is an excellent Christian attribute. The crow also has vision and the gift of prediction with intuitive powers going hand in hand with the gift of foresight. In Job 39, we find that the Eagle investigates the distance, which is exactly what the crows do on the roof of Knock Basilica. But Knock is not the only place where birds have a part of its spirituality. The Tower of London has six captive ravens to protect it. The raven and the crow are first cousins, if not a closer relationship. The Cathedral in Barcelona has 13 white geese to protect it from intruders and thieves. I love the reason for 13. When St. Eulalia was martyred during the reign of Diocletian, she was 13 and she was tortured by 13 different methods. The goose is a symbol of treasure, loyalty and protection.

And Knock has its crows in abundance. Next time you see the crow, think about its long symbolic history of intelligence, being fearless as we know only too well and the great mystery of creation.

The crow has a higher perspective than most other birds; it has the power of prophetic insight. My mindfulness prayer at the Gable Chapel ends like this. With the crows in mind, I look up to where Mary is looking with the prophet, 'Those with faith soar above the clouds' (Isaiah 40:31). Before I go to roost for the night, I seek out from all the birds of the air what they see that I cannot see, and to hear what they hear that I cannot hear.

Notwithstanding the fact that Fr. Richard Gibbons and the local people of Knock may well have different opinions of the crows of Connaught, I walk home in the assurance that these birds are safely roosting for the night in quiet contemplation in a nearby wood.

Good night to the praying crows of Knock.

Apparition Chapel

Sole to Soul – A Local Pilgrimage

A pilgrimage is more than simply a spiritual experience. It is an opportunity to harmonise with nature, enjoy dialogue with fellow beings and take in local history. What is more, it can happen on your doorstep.

On the BBC recently, Simon Reeve explored the meaning of pilgrimage as he retraced the footsteps of our ancestors from Holy Island in Northumberland to Jerusalem.

Pilgrimage has been deeply ingrained in the Christian psyche ever since 383 when the great Egeria went to Jerusalem and wrote about her experience. As a parish, we have done the Camino de Santiago de Compostela – or at least 100 miles of it; we have been to Rome, Jerusalem, Lourdes and Knock.

All these journeys produced different spiritual experiences for those who participated; but one thing they have in common is that the idea of pilgrimage to faraway places is attractive. Need that be an essential aspect of pilgrimage? When Pope Emeritus Benedict called for the Year of Faith, and encouraged us to go on pilgrimage, a few people in the parish decided to do a local one with the focus on nearby churches.

There is something profoundly simple about this. Walking around the churches in your neighbourhood enhances your knowledge of the district as you observe the beauty of gardens, houses, people, and historical sites, which are never seen from a car. The exercise itself and the dialogue with your fellow pilgrims place you firmly in harmony with nature. The space outside your parish may well be different from what lies within, and that needs to be acknowledged and prayed through

John O'Donohue, in *Eternal Echoes*, writes beautifully about the need in us to walk the field of the neighbour, for it is there that we experience the infinity of God and the magnificent freedom of nature. Walking the field of a neighbour's parish thrusts the pilgrim beyond a comfort zone, into another world which many people find spiritual.

Local places of pilgrimage Canterbury, Walsingham, Lindisfarne, and Iona – have served their purpose well in this respect. The goal of the pilgrimage matters little, but the communal effort to get there is supremely significant. If our goal is Heaven itself, then we need a daily reminder of those powerful words in the Magnificat, "to give knowledge of salvation to his people by the forgiveness of their sins …" (Luke 1:77). It was on one of our pilgrimages that I personally came to appreciate the beauty of that promise. A pilgrimage, no matter how short it may be, allows the secular to meet the sacred, the soles of the feet to meet the soul within, the body to meet the inner self.

With a local pilgrimage in mind, we took seven churches as found in the Book of Revelation and transferred the message of John to seven churches in our area. The aim, if possible, was to walk from one church to another or from one historical point to a church. The main purpose was to enable as many parishioners as possible to visit the seven churches. People could walk, cycle or drive to the designated building. We picked certain Sunday afternoons to highlight some aspects of the liturgical year. We used high days like Pentecost, Corpus Christi and the Birthday of Our Lady to ponder the meaning of the pilgrimage of life; and the seven pilgrimages were completed within the Year of Faith. When possible, we had food, sometimes at the start and sometimes at the end, and in a few cases at both. The pilgrimage always ended with a short liturgical service, organised by the host church.

There was fun, singing and praying – but most of all, there was an experience of sharing the journey of life. Running parallel to the pilgrimage for a period was the preparation of 45 candidates for the Sacrament of Confirmation.

The young people were encouraged to take part in the walks; they did so with enthusiasm and with a great keenness to share where they were on their faith journey. The interaction between the young people themselves and the adults was wonderful to experience. The young enjoyed the food, especially when it was available at both ends of the journey.

There was a strong ecumenical dimension to the pilgrimage through the involvement of two Anglican churches, whose communities turned out to welcome us. They offered hospitality and then we walked together to ponder the Scriptures of the particular feast day.

In the process, we learned a great deal of local history; in one case, we started off where Mass had been celebrated secretly in 1731, to retrace historical steps to the home of Blessed Margaret Pole, Countess of Salisbury, from where she was taken under house arrest in 1538.

The numbers turning out for each pilgrimage were most encouraging: as few as 45 people in poor weather up to 175 when it was fine, albeit cold. The interactions in conversation were remarkable as people encountered others they had never seen before, even though they were from the same parish, whilst some met friends whom they had not seen for years. I was amazed at the enthusiasm of the pilgrims: on at least two occasions I was opting for the easier journey, yet the group was determined to plough the tougher route.

On each pilgrimage, people were given a 'Pilgrim's Passport' which was ceremoniously stamped with the parish stamp of the host parish. Many took great delight in having their passport accredited with official approval. Only two people mentioned indulgences!

We were constantly reminded that in this life we are pilgrims, not tourists, and the difference between them is this: tourists complain, pilgrims praise.

Our prayer of praise was taken from an old Jewish prayer:

(Citation: GRUFFERTY, T. February 2014
The Tablet)

A prayer of praise

May the God who called our father Abraham to journey into the unknown and guarded him and blessed him, protect us too and bless our journey.

May his confidence support us as we set out.

May his spirit be with us on the way.

May he lead us back home in peace.

Those we love, we commend to his care. He is with them. We shall not fear.

As for us, may his presence be our companion so that blessings may come to us and everybody we meet.

Blessed are you God Almighty whose presence travels with his people.

What follows are some ideas we used in the Liturgies of the seven local Churches.

These days we talk about enlightened techno art on social media, but Caravaggio was ahead of the revolution of light with an enlightened mind. I stood spellbound for an exceptionally long time before St Jerome with his naked torso shining against the cardinal's hat.

Things to do.

- ❖ *Pick seven Churches in your locality.*
- ❖ *Read Revelation Chapters 2 -3.*
- ❖ *Try to match the seven scripture messages to the seven Churches.*
- ❖ *Pick seven significant days in the year.*
- ❖ *Go on pilgrimage.*

November to October Pilgrimage.
Pilgrimage to the Seven Churches

During one of the special years, (I think it was the Year of Faith), a group of us decided to use seven local Churches over the course of the Holy Year in imitation of the Pilgrimage as found in the Book of Revelation. You can travel any way you wish. There are opportunities to walk, cycle, use the car, or public transport. Collect your passport at any of the churches and make sure you have it stamped on each occasion.

Make sure you also take the message from Revelations to ponder in your heart. Each Church will provide a prayerful reflection of its own choice.

We explored and shared the history of the modern place of pilgrimage, for example Ephesus and we made a transfer to the church we were visiting. There were fascinating contributions from the members of that Church. We then read the scripture from Revelations, we had spontaneous prayers, and finished off with a blessing. We then shared food. The Confirmation Candidates and their parents loved the experience.

Ephesus: Revelation 2:1-7

A Sunday in November.

Ephesus is an ancient city situated on the major trade routes and a leading port in New Testament times. There were about 500,000 people who were Roman citizens. The major attraction even to this day is the Temple of Diana (Artemis) and is also reputed to be where Our Lady and St. John settled.

Smyrna: Revelation 2:8-11

A Sunday in January- Week of Prayer.

Smyrna is modern Izmir. This was famed for its street of gold with a temple at each end. It also boasted of a wealthy academic community and had a population of 200,000 in New Testament times.

Pergamum: Revelation 2:12-17

A Sunday in February

Pergamum was the capital of the Attalid Kingdom in the 3rd-2nd century BC. It housed the second largest library in the Roman Empire. There was a sacred Altar to Zeus and healings were practised.

Thyatira: Revelation 2:18-29

A Sunday in May

Thyatira is modern Akhisar because it was on the trade routes and had many trade guilds.

Sardis: Revelation 3:1-6

A Saturday in June with a Vigil Mass followed

by a shared social.

Sardis was destroyed by a great earthquake in AD17. It was rebuilt by the Emperor Tiberius. It was a wealthy fortress city built on a hill but easily accessed by the fertile river valley basin.

Philadelphia: Revelation 3:7-13
A Sunday in September

This was also destroyed by the earthquake of AD17 and rebuilt. It had one of the finest Hellenistic Educational centres.

Laodicea: Revelation 3:14-22
A Sunday in October.

This is modern Eski Hisar and it suffered two earthquakes during New Testament times. It produces world-famous black wool; it was the centre of banking and had a famous medical school.

May the God who called our father Abraham

to journey into the unknown,

and guarded him and blessed him

protect us too and bless our Pilgrimage.

May his confidence support us today.

May his spirit be with us on the way.

May he lead us back home in peace.

May his presence be our companion,

so that blessings may come to us,

to be inspired by the words and works

of Jesus Christ whose presence travels with us,

the Pilgrim People.

Amen

The Pilgrim Ways in Portsmouth Diocese

I want to pick up where I left off in the Summer Edition. There are at least two Pilgrim Ways crisscrossing large parts of Portsmouth Diocese. The most famous is between Winchester and Canterbury. A small group of us walked from Hastings to Winchester some years ago. There is no better view from the South Downs with the village of Amberley covered in an early morning mist, a spiritual experience and Morning Prayer all in one.

The actual way is prehistoric, but it became

famous when Thomas à Becket was canonised in 1173. Until the dissolution of the monasteries, the South Downs Way was indeed popular with the pilgrims going to the tomb of Becket. Today it takes you right through the South Downs National Park with super scenery and wildlife. I deliberately used the word 'crisscross' because an equally famous Pilgrim Way went from the North of England to the South Coast. This is known as the Way of St. James. Pilgrims used Reading as a stop- over. They made the final stages of their journey towards the South Coast to cross the English Channel from Brighton, Portsmouth, Southampton, and Poole. As they drew near to the Pyrenees, excitement would have mounted considerably. Seven of us walked the last 100 miles from Ponferrada to Santiago in 2003. Arrival at the famous Cathedral must be one of the most anticipated experiences in Christendom. I would encourage you to watch the Film *The Way* and then set out on the journey of a lifetime especially if you are young at heart. There is no better welcome in the entire world than the open doors of the Cathedral in Santiago de Compostela.

Talking of 'Open Doors' reminds me of the Year of Mercy just starting. You could do something incredibly special by organising a pilgrimage to the two appointed places of Prayer in our Diocese for this special year. St. John's Cathedral and the Church of Our Lady and St. Edmund, Abingdon will have Holy Doors for the year. Pope Francis writes beautifully about the Open Door of the Church as a sign that the door to the Father is always open. He points out that as well as opening inwards the door also opens outwards. We are sent out at every Mass to share faith and witness to the Good News.

(Citation: GRUFFERTY, T. Autumn 2015 *Portsmouth People*)

Young Peoples' Spiritual Dynamism on Pilgrimage

It is a well-documented fact that many young people from good Catholic homes no longer engage in any kind of Church events, and most of all in Mass. In the last ten years, a great number of parents have commented about the fact that their children have lapsed from the faith. Many of our young parents refuse to have their children baptised and rarely set foot in church, even for family celebrations. I heard of an incredibly sad occasion recently when two children did not attend their father's Requiem Mass. Instead, they followed the funeral cortège from the Church to the cemetery. Many parents are traumatised about the situation and blame themselves with serious recriminations. It is the most frequent topic of discussion among many Catholic parents.

As a priest, I struggle to comfort these concerned parents and often say that, if they are good people, then they have been good parents. That never seems to be an adequate explanation nor a consolation to these distressed Catholics. While I was in Ireland this summer, I took a keener interest than normal in young people engaged in religion. I must point out that I was surprised at what I found.

Young people may not be in the church pew but that does not mean they are not engaged in Church events. These are three examples. I was at the afternoon Mass in Knock Basilica on July 22nd this year. At the beginning of Mass, we were invited to welcome many people who had walked to Knock from the four corners of Ireland, Belfast, Derry, Dublin, Cork. They were members of the Cursillo movement.

I would think that more than a third of the group were under 30 years. After Mass, I spoke to the pilgrims from Derry. I asked one young man how many times he had walked from Derry, he proudly said '14 Times'. When I remarked he must have been young when he started, he added he was 28. After further discussion he said he would do the pilgrimage every year for as long as he was able. He went on to highlight what he got out of the experience. These are the spiritual benefits he gained: **renewal of faith in God, in people, in the beauty of creation, but, above all, he gained a new self-appreciation of who he was as a person from the solidarity of walking with others and the welcome they received on the 127-mile journey.**

I stood back to observe the interaction between these 130 people following their Mass in the renovated old church. They were vibrant, they had joy, they obviously enjoyed each other's company, they were in real contact with each other. I wondered to myself when was the last time we saw such enthusiastic interaction after Mass on Sunday? All these people had enthusiasm, joy and a profound sense of idealism that needs to be acknowledged and affirmed by the Church. I really admire how Fr. Richard Gibbons and the community at Knock welcomed those people.

Staying with Knock, I noticed another group of young people at the weekends with high visibility jackets. These are a group of 20 secondary school young people who help around the Shrine. They arrive on Friday night, stay in the youth hostel and return to their homes on Sunday evening. They are trained on what to do, but especially in welcoming people to the Shrine. Over two weekends, I spoke to several of these volunteers and that they were full of confidence on who they are, delighted to help, smiling, and dedicated to their tasks for the weekend.

Again, I stood back to observe what these young people were doing. I watched their zeal, their charm and enthusiasm. There was a strong sense of envy as I thought to myself: 'I need six of these people in my parish before and after Mass every Sunday'. Just because people have stopped going to Mass, it does not mean that they have lost their spiritual dynamism or their idealism. I was personally encouraged that all is not lost with the modern generation. However, we do need to observe where they are coming from and respond with enthusiasm, with a fiery passion for the Good News in whatever situation we may find it. Barbara Brown Taylor writes beautifully about the thin place between earth and heaven. There are numerous moments each day when the curtain is opened even for a second so that we can see beyond- 'This place that has made us Kin'.

Homilies

Sermon for Fr. David Freeman:
Requiem St. Patrick's Hayling Island June 2016.

'I am the Way, the Truth and the Life' (John 14:6).

A priest who preaches in the presence of his bishop, and especially his fellow priests, must be very holy, or incredibly wise, or very foolish.

In Chartres Cathedral, there is a wonderful statue of Melchizedek ...probably the only image of the King and Priest of Salem. When I first saw the statue, I was reminded of David Freeman. The statue is thin, small, and rather severe looking. However, there is no cigarette in Melchizedek's hand.

But the physical likeness between David and the mysterious Melchizedek is not the only relationship. There is a spiritual affinity too. When David left us in the seventies, he came back with an intense self-questioning and sadness. Looking back now, there should have been something in place to enrich his priesthood and cushion him back to full-time ministry. Sadly, he never recovered emotionally from the experience.

But the spiritual conviction that he was a priest forever was very strong- a priest forever, according to the order of Melchizedek (Psalm110:4, Hebrews 7:17). At the heart of that conviction was the great gift of fidelity.

Fidelity must be one of the chief characteristics of a priest's life. If he found Melchizedek his inspiration for fidelity, he found Jesus as the Way, the Truth and the Life (John 14:6).

If Jesus promised to be the Way, David followed

him, through thick and thin. He found wonderful signposts directing him to Jesus in his pastoral ministry and in celebrations of the sacraments. David was keenly aware that Jesus the Way is the way of Love. I know from my involvement in this community that you could but not but love the people of this parish, with their beautiful island mentality. David's love was often seen as he cycled round the Island administering the Sacrament of the Sick or giving Holy Communion to the sick and the housebound. His bike had a special black box for the oils. Only on Hayling does the 'black box' take on a new meaning.

It would be remiss of me not to mention Elizabeth, David's housekeeper for many years, his friends here in Hayling especially Tom and Margaret, Mary and Frank who lovingly cared for him these last few months. I would like to highlight the special care David received from his priest colleagues, especially Fr. Gerard Flynn and Lesley Adams and Rajesh. In the Priests' Retirement Fund, we have a conviction that the best care our retired priests receive comes from the local Church, the priests, and lay people of the Parish. If love was the driving force of David's life, the truth of the Good News also played a significant part in David's quest, especially in the last 20 years. He had a fundamental desire for the lies of life to be turned into truth, that fiction became fact. He had a passion for truth, and he knew only too well that the truth of Jesus made him free. The truth of Jesus always frees us from bondage. David's liberation into truth came fully in death, as it will do for each of us.

In the promise of Jesus being the Life, it must be said that David did not really enjoy life as much as he should have done. Rarely if ever, did he take the high road, as life for him was drudgery.

That should be a lesson to us all. Life is good and, for us believers, there is the promise of life in abundance.

Enjoy every moment and ponder the Promises of Jesus.

For David Freeman, there is most certainly unfinished business, but I am convinced the promise of life in abundance will be the process whereby he will enjoy eternity to the full of Jesus as the Way, the Truth and the Life.

He may well have been given the opportunity to have a glass of the best Scottish with Melchizedck in one of those ensuite rooms mentioned by Jesus in the Gospel today.

I doubt very much if David will be able to smoke, as that is solely reserved for the place below!

May his soul smile to the lives of those he served as a priest.

Maurice Twomey R.I.P. 1932 – 2010
Requiem St. Peter's Winchester

Fr Maurice Twomey will be astonished that so many of us are here this afternoon and there might be even some in-depth analysis on why we are here. We have come to say farewell, to pay tribute and pray for his gentle soul. On his behalf, I thank you for your presence and your prayer for a dear friend. I would also like to thank those who cared for Maurice in the final years of his life, people like Claire McKenna from this Parish, but others too. He might not have said so, but he appreciated your visits and help. Maurice was of noble stock but lived in a modest way. I was always surprised at the starkness of his immediate surroundings. What he lacked in home comforts he was rich with intellect and a great storyteller ...a shanachie (Irish old-fashioned storyteller) in the traditional folklore of his native country.

As he told his stories, Maurice added the wisdom of Joyce, the earthiness of Brendan Behan and the sublime beauty of W.B. Yeats. I am not at all sure he was aware of what he was doing for they, and others, were in his DNA.

As was politics, which rarely got aired. There were two things that shaped Maurice's life, and these stayed with him right to the end.

Annie Curran his Godmother left him a great gift in her will. Maurice was to spend three months in Paris soaking up the French Culture and Language. He did so in such a fashion that the wonderful present remained with him for the rest of his days.

We belonged to a walking group. Brian Murphy O'Connor was surprised to find we were in a rather dubious section of Paris and Maurice guided five celibate priests through the Moulin Rouge without any one of us having to do the Can Can!

The second thing he relished were his days as a seminarian at Heythrop College. Bishop Worlock made a wise decision to send Maurice into the world of academia because he was well able to hold his own with the intellectuals of the theological world. Out of those days grew a great love for Mother Church. In his heyday, Maurice was the most informed priest. I often thought that I was first with a snippet of news, only to discover that Maurice knew already. He would then namedrop to make doubly sure that what I knew he knew, and he knew it before me.

It was often said that long before Bishop Crispian asked a priest from one parish to move to another, Maurice knew where he was going.

Maurice laboured long and hard in pastoral work, and sometimes that did not come easy. He loved his time in Horndean, mainly because the people there contributed to and enhanced his ministry. I see encouraging signs where lay people are more than willing to complement the leadership role of their priest. Maurice might well have trail-blazed a new trend.

Out of Heythrop too came a great desire to be a good priest. Our two New Testament readings today are taken from the Rite of Ordination deliberately and with good purpose. If Paul asks Timothy to be to all believers an example in the way you speak and behave, in your love, your faith and in your purity, Maurice most certainly tried his hardest to exercise those priestly characteristics.

There are lay people here today and priests who are active members of our Diocese because of the dedication and commitment of Maurice.

Long before Facebook, Maurice had a network of people from across the country. These appear to be men and women who saw in him the true marks of what it means to be a servant of the Lord Jesus Christ.

The best members of Maurice's network were his

sister Myra and her husband John. He loved to visit Devon, mainly because of you and your children. He would arrive in Devon with quizzes that kept the children entertained for hours. He never told anybody that his nieces and nephew called him 'Uncle Mew'.

St Paul in our scriptures says that he was a prisoner of the Lord. Maurice too was a prisoner in his self-doubt and low self-esteem.

Death itself was the great liberator. Maurice has been set free from the Bars and the Chains that have kept him fettered for the last 17 years. Following a great labour of love, Maurice has discovered, as we shall all discover, that Jesus is the Way, the Truth, and the Life.

When Jesus says that there are many rooms in my Father's House (John 14:2), I pray that all the rooms are ensuite for Maurice Twomey's sake and for ours. If Maurice was a Francophile by adoption, he was a true son of the Celts and he would want me to say these words for his gentle soul:

May you have a wonderful welcome in the home you are going to.

May you have a wonderful urgency to live eternity to the full.

May the Resurrection of Jesus transfigure everything that is negative in you and about you.

May your soul smile in the embrace of your Anam Cara

The Woman at the Well

Come and dip your hand in the water but do nothing.

Why did the Samaritan woman come to draw water at noon, the hottest time of the day?

Did she want to avoid the times the other women in town came to the well?

We are invited to the well. Sit on the wall.

Ponder on the meeting between this woman and Jesus.

The well itself is deeply symbolic. It is a meeting place for young people. Young men came here to water the cattle and young women came for water for the house. This is how Rebecca and Rachel met their husbands. So, this place is a place of romance.

John does not miss the point because just before this story, he has Jesus talk about the bride and groom.

It is also full of history. This well belonged to Jacob, the grandson of Abraham. He gives the well to his son Joseph. He who controls the well controls the town, especially in arid climates.

So, this woman comes to the well at midday. Notice she is young. Hardly a woman with five husbands, unless she had them in quick succession. She gazes into the well. She is alone.

The well is dark and deep, symbolizing her spiritual state. She is framed in the midday sun. Jesus is about to cast more light on her. Notice how quickly she changes the subject when Jesus becomes personal. She does acknowledge the exposure by saying: 'I see you are a prophet'.

What are the places in my life where I am embarrassed, where I avoid interaction with others?

What are the noonday wells of my life? Can I imagine Jesus approaching me there? Jesus tries to reveal

His thirst to her - perhaps His thirst for intimacy with her - but she puts Him off. She is not worthy. It won't work. When He offers to satisfy her thirst, she puts Him off. He cannot satisfy what she needs, at least with this well, and without a bucket.

How do I put Jesus off - with excuses, with problems, with barriers? I do not have time; I haven't done this before; my stuff's too complicated; I don't know how to find you in this mess. When He shows her that He knows her, she knows she is in the presence of someone special - perhaps the one she has thirsted for all her life.

Do I let Jesus show me that He knows and understands me?

Can I find the words to say:'He is the one I have thirsted for all my life?'

The grace will come when I see that I have been at the well a long time and have long been thirsty. When I can name the new thirst, the Water that now satisfies that thirst, I can overcome my remaining resistance to trust. When I see that Jesus reveals Himself to me by revealing me to me, thereby showing me my need for Him as Saviour, I will rejoice and tell the whole world, too.

Now look at the reflection in the water. There are two people -the Woman and Jesus. She appears to be much older this time.

She came alone but she is now no longer alone. She has met the One and, through Him, she has met the other people in her Sychar. She came alone, but now she returns to the town without her water, to tell them of the One she had met. They too no longer rely on her word; they have encountered Jesus too

A Wedding Homily

I am delighted that Edward and Victoria have chosen Paul's letter to the Corinthians as one of the Readings for their wedding. It must be one of the greatest pieces of writing and a recipe for the whole of life.

There was once a chap called Edward who had an immensely powerful dream. The dream told him that if he went to the financial district of London, he would find a real treasure that would bring complete happiness for the rest of his days.

The dream was so strong that he got on the train. He spent the whole day around the Bank of England looking at people, buildings and even down at the street. Evening came and he had found no treasure. Even though he was starving, he continued his quest into the night and beyond midnight. He walked round and round, so much so that he came to the notice of the police.

Two officers approached him, asked him what he was looking for. He told them of his vivid dream.

One of the officers was particularly scornful and he said that he had dreams, but he would never follow them. Then he added that last night he had a dream of a real treasure about a young woman in Hampshire called Victoria, but he would never dream of going down to Havant to find her,

Suddenly the penny dropped. Edward got the earliest morning train back to his real treasure.

You see, sometimes the really important things in life are under our very noses.

We think that the excitements are in faraway places. That is precisely what Paul is saying. We are nothing without love. Love is patient and kind. Consider a kitchen with patience and kindness-there would be no need for the Great British Bake Off!

Love is never jealous, boastful, or conceited.

Consider our Law Courts - there would be no need for Judges and Juries or Divorce. Love is never selfish, does not take offence or is resentful.

I know the loveliest couple who have ever walked the face of the earth. They are many years married. On their wedding day, they opted never to do selfishness, take offence or be resentful. The thing is that their special qualities have spread to their children and beyond.

Paul goes on: 'Love takes not pleasure in other people sins'. Consider that alone for the moment, most of our lives are taken up with the downfall of the other.

But he keeps the best until the last .... 'love does not come to an end.'..the wedding ring is a powerful symbol of the everlasting qualities of love ....the ring has no beginning ...no end.

Somebody said that there are three rings in marriage:

The engagement ring

The wedding ring

And the Suffering........but even with suffering Edward and Victoria you will endure anything with love.

25th Sunday of the Year September

On the 25th Sunday of the Year I preached this sermon because, on the previous Wednesday, we had 1 Corinthians 12:31-13:13. It has always surprised me that we do not have this lovely reading at a Sunday Liturgy.

Burt Bacharach released a famous song in 1965 with these words, What the World needs now is LOVE, SWEET LOVE.

The writer of the lyrics may well have been inspired by the Second Reading today. Paul's description of love must be the greatest piece ever written about love.

I am going to highlight three profound things he says.

'Love is always Patient'. If an Eskimo were to walk into your life at this moment would she find that your love was always patient? The real test for my patience is in the checkout queue in Tesco. Usually, this is what I think: 'I've picked the worse queue'. Then the real test comes when the old man immediately in front of me has checked out all his groceries and he tells the assistant that he has forgotten the milk and the wife will kill him. You can well guess where Tom Grufferty is going on this one.

Love Is Always Patient.
Love Is Always Trusting.

The other day we had the feast of St. John Bosco, who founded the Salesians. He is the greatest teacher of all time, due mainly to his trust of those in his care. His main policy was to let the pupils be themselves, to trust them.

If You Trust People, They Will Be Trusting. If You Believe In People, They Will

Believe In Themselves. Trust Your Fellow-Parishioners and They Will Flourish.

We must be cautious about controlling others. The Church loves to control.

The Final one is: *Love Is Always Hopeful.*

For the last two years, nearly everyone in this country is driven to despair and pessimism. It pervades our media; it is on every page of our newspapers. I am afraid to say that our religious leaders are caught in the trap of hopelessness as well.

Let there be one beacon of Hope here in Liss today.

Let everyone walk out of here full of Hope. Let us get up tomorrow morning saying that Monday 4th February will be a good day. I checked out the *Oxford Thesaurus* on hope and I found the following: 'confidence, aspiring, positive, buoyant, anticipation, promise, faith, assurance, yearning, ambition, heartening' - that is only ten, there are several others, but the challenge is, will any of us have any of those dispositions in the coming days?

What the World needs now is Love.

Who are the 72 Disciples?

For the last ten days we have been treated to the most psychodrama the likes of which we have not seen on Coronation Street, EastEnders or even the Archers. Added to that, we have had four months of depression, pessimism and fear. All not at all helped by England being knocked out of Europe in more ways than one.

The Lord sends out 72 disciples to evangelise and they come back rejoicing because people notice what they are doing. I know this word 'evangelisation' is a big word and few of us understand it.

I was in Bath the other day and near the door of the Abbey Church, was a large sign with the word 'Healing' on it. There were several people praying with, and for, people who needed healing. These were the 72 disciples of our time.

We had the primary school leavers' Mass the other evening. I asked Year 6 what the best thing was they had learned during their seven years in school. There were some wonderful responses but the best one was: 'I learned that mistakes are OK, provided one learns from them'. That child is one of the 72 disciples of our time. She is evangelising her parents, her teachers and peers.

You see, being sent and doing takes as many shapes as there are people. You live your Christianity differently to me and to everyone else here. Pope Francis is very clear on this. We are not all peas in the pod; we are different. Your way of loving others will be different to mine. Your way of hope will be different to the person sitting beside you. Your ways of Faith will be different to mine - no less authentic and no less effective to anyone else.

If everyone here was to leave Mass today full of Optimism and Hope, we would make a vast difference to our world. We would become the 72 disciples in this place right now.

Despite what befalls us, we must be people of Hope because our calling and our destiny are wonderful.

Jesus says the Harvest is rich. Life is indeed rich, and once you start sharing in the riches, people begin to see things differently.

A priest walks his dog every day and every day he meets a fellow dog-walker. His fellow dog-walker is pessimistic - every morning there is something awful about life and the weather,

Then one morning there is beautiful sunshine and warm weather and the priest wonders what the reaction will be when he meets his friend. Sure, enough there is no change. When they meet his friend says: 'We had an awful day yesterday'.

Do you really want to be one of the 72 disciples? Then, for you the bottle is always half-full and never half-empty.

The Fig Tree

On the Sunday with the Gospel about the Fig Tree, I preached on the significance of the fig, with emphasis that, on planting, the tree does not produce fruit for three years. The following Sunday, a lovely lady presented me with two jars of Fig Jam with these words: 'I give the impression that I don't give a fig, but I do, and these jam pots prove the point'.

Parishioners surprise priests daily! Thank God.

The Parish and Church as a Family
Family Happiness

During July 2013 in an interview with the Argentinian weekly, *Viva*, Pope Francis listed 10 tips to find greater happiness in family life today.

Louise Casey, the Director General of the Government's troubled Family Programme, has revealed that society in Britain is heading for a shipwreck because of increasing difficulties in family life. She claims that the results of the breakdown in family life could cost the country an extra £1,500 per taxpayer per year. It seems we face a giant tsunami of social problems unless we take measures immediately. The Churches have a positive contribution to make to the creation of good family life. The Synod on "Pastoral Challenges to the Family in the Context of Evangelisation" is currently taking place in Rome. It is a great opportunity for us to re-assess and acknowledge the invaluable riches of families in parish life. It is also an opportunity to examine the nature of the family and what it needs in terms of support from parishes, as those difficulties in family life alluded to by Casey are not by any means foreign to families in the average Catholic parish. The top 10 secrets to happiness recently given to us by Pope Francis can be easily applied to healthy family living in the parish.

BE GIVING of yourself to others. Generosity is one of the greatest blessings parents and grandparents bestow. Our response as children to that generosity is often very inconsistent. Think of those elderly people in nursing homes who seem to be gradually forgotten, with fewer and fewer visits.

These are the very people who nourished us into life, when death comes, everybody flocks like crows to a piece of rubbish. Our elderly are not rubbish, and we all need to acknowledge their profound contribution to our family heritage and culture.

PROCEED CALMLY. One of the great pressures on family life today is stress. We are pressured to do better in every aspect of life from our first day of school. We need to develop a calmness of life that includes prayer and reflection, to remind us regularly who we are and what is our destiny.

DEVELOP A HEALTHY SENSE of leisure. That "all Work and no play makes Jack a dull boy" is a truth at the highest level. I am currently on sabbatical, which gives me a great opportunity to calmly observe the life of those around me. I have started my four months away in the west of Ireland. One thing that has struck me about family life here is families playing together, even at Mass. The family that plays together stays together – as does the family that prays together.

SUNDAYS SHOULD BE HOLIDAYS. God gave us the Sabbath for rest and for honouring His blessings, but for many people the seven days of the week are indistinguishable. Sabbath time is crucial, and we should remember that it comes every seven days. I am having an extended Sabbath - so when was the last time you asked your priest if he wanted to have a sabbatical? The Sunday liturgy presents every parish with great opportunities to celebrate family life.

The family needs a much higher profile at the Sunday Eucharist. To name one Mass a "Family Mass" is a serious misnomer, for every Mass has to be a family occasion. How many parishes have a different family to take the collection each Sunday?

In my last parish we had a gifted motivator who visited the First Holy Communion parents once per year to encourage the parents and children to take responsibility for welcoming people to Mass. Every year he received an excellent response. That developed into families composing and saying the bidding prayers.

There is something very profound about a child leading a prayer when they have only just learned to read! And…we found the smaller the child praying, the bigger the prayerful response from the congregation. Pentecost was always special as prayers were prayed in different languages. Here, the parish was highlighting the fact that it is a family with worldwide dimensions and speaking in many tongues. Try to involve families of different nationalities directly in the liturgy. Perhaps have a reading in Polish one Sunday and in Tagalog the next.

FIND NEW WAYS to create dignified jobs for young people. The necessity of having meaning and dignity in a person's job goes without saying but sadly it rarely happens, especially with young people, and when people move in and out of work opportunities rather than staying in one job all their life. Pray for young people every Sunday.

RESPECT AND CARE FOR NATURE. Several times in the past few months I have seen families exploring creation together. Garden centres provide an outing for the whole family. I have also seen families gardening together, each with their own tasks that are appropriate for their age and strength.

DON'T BE NEGATIVE. There is sometimes a serious shortage of praise in family life. Self-esteem can be at a low ebb. Parents need to stand four-square beside all their children regardless of what career they have chosen or who they have married or live with. When did you last praise your children for just being wonderful? They must be wonderful, because they are created in the image and likeness of God - and in your image and likeness too,

RESPECT OTHERS' BELIEFS. We have moved a very long way in accepting other Christians as fellow believers. Having worked with Churches Together for many years I know that we still have a great deal to learn from our fellow Christians, just as they can profit from our rich resources. We also need to go the extra mile with other faiths.

WORK FOR PEACE. There is a new peace bridge across the river Foyle in Derry (Londonderry). It is a potent symbol of what can be achieved between divided communities, but real peace is in the hearts of people.

FORGIVENESS. This brings us full circle, Pope Francis' first secret of happiness ties with the last recipe for family happiness. This is the greatest and the most needed requirement in my family and in its history. I wager that it is also the most outstanding need in yours also. Out of the reconciliation and forgiveness of family memories and hurts will come the inner tranquillity only the Lord can give.

(Citation: **GRUFFERTY, T** October 2014. *The Tablet*)

Parish Echoes

As you would expect Parish Ministry has been a huge feature in my life for the last 47 years. The following Echoes are a small selection of all the wonderful thigs that I have encountered, at the heart of all these Echoes are people, faith and love.

Both ends of Life

How to celebrate a baptism and a funeral at the same time.

Anna gave birth to a healthy boy. Eight weeks after the birth of her firstborn, Anna developed stomach pains. She was diagnosed with a tumour in the liver which was a secondary cancer from an original lump in her breast. Anna began an intensive course of chemotherapy. This was due to last for two months. Three weeks into the chemotherapy treatment. Anna died, leaving a 13week-old baby, a heart broken husband, her parents, family and friends.

When Edmund, the young husband, came to arrange the funeral. he said the family did not want a Requiem Mass as Anna was not a Catholic. He was not certain what funeral rites we did in the absence of Mass but whatever we did should include the baptism of their son, also called Edmund. I was taken aback at the vigour of the request. I had misgivings about what the liturgical experts` might say. Something about St Paul`s dying and rising flashed through my mind. Immediately, I was drawn to the scriptures for the rite of baptism and found St Paul`s profound description of our baptism as a sharing in Christ`s death and resurrection. I read Romans 6:3-5 to Edmund and his sister, who had come with him to arrange the funeral.

"You know that when we go to Christ, we are all baptised and plunged into his death. By his baptism we are buried with Christ, and, as Christ was raised from

among the dead by the glory of the Father, so we must walk in a new life. We have been buried with him to share in his death, in a symbolic way: and so, we will share in his resurrection". Romans 6:3-5.

Without any hesitation. All three of us were convinced that this had to be the main reading for our liturgy. Never had the scriptures spoken so powerfully to me. On the strength of St Paul, I was 100 per cent certain that it was the right thing to do. But while we agreed that the ceremonies would go ahead as requested, I was still uncertain about how both ceremonies could be dovetailed. I explained my predicament to a priest friend. Fr Tom Taaffe. who emailed me about the connection between the waters of baptism and the holy water we use in the funeral rites. So, the funeral rites had to be in the context of baptism - especially because the deceased mother was herself baptised. It was exactly the link - and the assurance- which I needed to proceed. Once I had made that connection, I found all kinds of other associations between baptism and funeral rites, between birth and death. My apprehensiveness disappeared and I began to look forward to a very special liturgy.

The day for the 'funeral in the context of baptism` arrived. The church was full of family. friends and relatives of Anna and Edmund, including Anna`s parents and Edmund's father. There were some parishioners too. We received the coffin at the church door, but without the sprinkling. This was omitted until after the child was baptised, to emphasise that baptism is the gateway into eternity.

As Anna`s coffin was carried into the church, Edmund followed immediately carrying his baby son in his arms. The child was tenderly and beautifully carried, it was one of the most emotive entrance processions I have ever experienced. There was not a dry eye in the church. It was the essence of a tender love for the child and the young mother who had died. In my introduction. I connected Anna's baptism with the beginning of her journey into eternity and what we were about to do for Edmund as he began his journey towards eternity. Then, at the Baptismal Front, with Anna's coffin alongside, we welcomed Edmund with the Sign of the Cross, which was done by the father, godparents, and grandparents.

The godparents were encouraged to fill the gap in this child's life occasioned by the death of his mother. The real reasons for sponsors unfolded before our very eyes as powerfully as never before. They acknowledged their role immediately and were willing to respond to that beautiful question: 'Are you willing to help the father of this child in his duty as a Christian parent? `

The reader proclaimed the reading from Romans with conviction and meaning. You could see the congregation making the link for themselves. It was a sweet moment to savour and it called for a long pause before the Psalm. The Gospel was John 3:1-6. with its emphasis on what is born of flesh being flesh and what is born of spirit being spirit. Then Edmund spoke movingly about his wife, with young Edmund in his arms, he related the bravery of Anna. Especially in the final weeks of her life. Instead of enjoying her new-born baby she was preparing for death which took place on the tenth anniversary of the couple's wedding.

He showed magnificent courage (and the child was perfectly behaved). The immediate family then moved to the Baptismal Font which fortunately is at the front of the Church. The assembly could see and participate. We called on the communion of saints including St Anna and St Edmund. Once Edmund was baptised, Edmund senior and I went to sprinkle Anna's coffin with the holy water from the font in which her son was just baptised. I pointed out that in the normal funeral rites we use holy water at least three times when the remains are received into the church, at the words of farewell at the graveside. This helped to emphasise that by water and the Holy Spirit we gain access into eternity. When it came to light the candle for the newly baptised, it was easy to see the strong link we make with the paschal candle at the Easter Vigil and the use of the candle at every baptism and funeral in the church. We often take this for granted.

Nobody would think of holding funeral rites without the paschal candle and yet it is rarely referenced. I am sure many people not familiar with Catholic liturgy wonder why the Easter candle is there. To illustrate the powerful symbolism. We dipped Edmund's candle three times in the water with these words taken from the liturgy of the Easter Vigil: "May all who are buried with Christ in the death of Baptism rise also with Him to newness of life..." Immediately we returned to position ourselves around Anna's coffin for the Bidding Prayers. For the final words of farewell, 1 used John O'Donohue's 'Blessing for the dead' (from *Anam Cara* p. 278) adapted for the occasion. I explained the meaning of "Anam Cara" and said that Anna was now a 'soul friend' to her only child in a way nobody had foreseen or expected.

Following the final commendation and farewell we carried Anna's coffin from the church with the final hymn: 'Lord of all Hopefulness". Directly behind the coffin was her husband and the newest Christian in the community, followed by godparents, grandparents, and the rest of the congregation.

There is a wonderful sequel to this story. On Remembrance Sunday we had a long tradition to gather to pray for all our deceased in Warblington Cemetery. About 12 years after Edmund's Baptism, I became aware of a father and son standing at the grave of Anna. It was one of the sweetest encounters I have ever had in a cemetery. May all our dead rest in peace.

(Citation: GRUFFERTY, T April 2003 Intercom Magazine)

Church of all the talents
Matthew 25:14-30

Our parishioners were a little shocked at Mass recently when, instead of asking them to donate money for some reason, I offered to give them money during the homily. After proclaiming the Gospel of the day - the parable of the talents (Matthew 25:14-30) 33rd Sunday Year A, I asked 40 people to accept £5 each representing the person in the parable who had been given five talents. I then asked 40 other people to accept £2 each - each representing the person who had been given two talents; and finally, 40 more people were offered £1 each.

They were encouraged not to bury their talent. (I then asked the parishioners not to contact Bishop Crispian Hollis to say that one of his priests had taken leave of his senses.)

Parishioners who were given the talents were invited to consider the credit crunch we are experiencing but, more importantly they were invited to use their talents for the benefit of the people of the Democratic Republic of the Congo - and I said that all the profits (together with the £320 I had distributed) would be donated to CAFOD.

All the talents were given on trust; no names were taken, and the money was given to anyone who was willing to accept it irrespective of age. People who were not fortunate enough to receive talents were also invited to get involved.

The idea was initially inspired by the Gospel itself, but it was tried out in the context of being a Stewardship Community, which we became last Lent. The essence of stewardship is that everybody in the parish is called to follow Jesus more closely and imitate his way of life. Stewardship is Trinitarian in that it stands on three great

Ts, Time, **Treasure and Talent**. Without the stewardship background, I doubt that I would have had the confidence to offer the challenge; because of it, I could not resist in pushing the boat.

I knew that the parishioners would rise to the occasion and respond with generosity and enthusiasm. Almost immediately the talents began to accumulate. As soon as one parishioner returned to her seat with her five talents a blind parishioner had pushed £10 into her hand.

Stories of ingenuity spread like wildfire around the parish immediately after Mass. Ciaran, aged 11, made special soft drinks, and with permission from his school, he sold the drinks to his classmates, his five talents became £75. Coffee mornings featured largely as the adults used their talents with one morning realising £175.

Even though no one in the parish choir had received any talents, they invited everyone to a sing-along of Christmas carols with refreshments and competitions. They raised £250 and have been asked to make this an annual event in the parish because people enjoyed themselves so much.

William, aged five, made a wide selection of cakes and set up a stall after Mass selling everything in no time - producing £125 with his one talent. One couple decided not to give each other Christmas gifts this year; instead, they gave a generous donation to CAFOD of what they probably would have spent on their gifts.

Our parish primary school head teacher organised sponsored spelling competition and the children contributed for the privilege of joining in.

In a short article such as this, I cannot include all the good examples of fundraising we had; but I do want to say that one of the things that amazed me was how much people wanted to participate. Two parishioners who are away from the parish on the Sunday when the talents were distributed, came to me asking for their talents when they returned.

I expected a twofold return on the original investment of £320 but we collected £5,063 for the Catholic charity. This was an increase of more than one 1,500 per cent on the original investment. No bank or financial institution offers such a return for money, and it shows how generous and how talented people are when they are so engaged. The most encouraging aspect of the entire exercise was to experience how people got involved, how they mixed with each other in new ways and how they thought up new initiatives.

One outstanding feature was to see how enthusiastic the children and young people were about using their talents for the good of others. The exercise also revealed how people, who are normally reluctant to tell others what they are actually good at, were keen to reveal how they had made their money when it came to talk about the return on their dividends.

Our parish has a long history of people being involved in a wide range of ministries with a strong emphasis on social activities. Not everybody wants to be a Reader or an Extraordinary Minister of Holy Communion at Mass, and not everyone is cut out to be a catechist ~ but most people can sell cakes at the summer fair or set a table for an Alpha Supper.

In the process of becoming a Stewardship Community we identified 55 fundamental needs in our community ~ some more important than others, some needed only from time to time. We are now in the process of finding people who can use their talents to respond to those needs. We are doing this by asking people to address the congregation on different ministries once a month on what we call "ministry Sunday" - inviting people to sign up if they think their talents fit the need. For example, one of the needs that emerged was to improve our contact with the wider community.

A letter was prepared saying who we are, where the church is and when it is open for quiet prayer. It offers to pray for all the recipients of the letter the following Sunday at Mass. Two women now deliver 100 letters each week to households in the parish.

The feedback from this initiative has been most encouraging. Several people have phoned to say that our prayers are appreciated or that the letter arrived at a low time in their lives and it helped them.

What happened in our parish was remarkable - not because of the money that was raised and not because of the talents that were discovered and used to raise the money - but because people related to the Gospel in a particular and profound way in their ordinary lives. Week after week, we hear and reflect on the Gospel, but we need help to make the connection with our individual and community lives. In this instance, it worked.

(Citation: GRUFFERTY, T. January 2009.*The Tablet*)

The Parish without FOOD

Pope Francis often talks about the Parish with the family as being remarkably similar, but the parallel only goes so far. Any family facing a future without food would consider itself doomed to starving to death from malnutrition. Every family must have food. However, the habits of sharing that essential have changed in our time.

The Parish Family faces an immediate future without the spiritual sustenance of the Eucharist. Most priests in England and Wales are over 60 years old which means that in ten years' time there is going to be a cosmic change for those who wish to gather around the table of the Lord. No food for the journey means eventually, death by slow starvation. That in turn means that our efforts at Evangelisation are a waste of time because we are not going to be able to feed ourselves, never mind those people we expect to join us.

The amalgamation of parishes only serves to prolong the lingering death. Unless the Holy Spirit and Pope Francis have a plan?

Parish without a Priest

For several months, I have been doing weekend supply work in a parish where the priest suddenly announced that he could no longer cope with the pressures of modern-day pastoral life. He was parish priest in this parish for eight years – a parish with two modern churches (formerly two parishes) in a well-to-do part of Hampshire. Both parishes have had a good record of having good priests without historical baggage and the parish has the ministry of two permanent deacons who are outstanding leaders.

The priest who announced his sudden departure was dearly loved by his parishioners and got on well with his fellow priests. There was a maximum involvement of laity right across every aspect of parish life. It is an understatement to say that these people were in a state of shock at the departure of their priest. As an outsider coming in every weekend, three issues emerged: How do you grieve for someone you have the highest regard for? How do you cope without a full-time resident priest? And how can we exercise our baptismal calling? It is fascinating to listen and observe how these people are addressing these concerns. Addressing the third concern first, and without any professional recommendations or prompting, they began to carry out their parish ministries with greater enthusiasm than ever. Our laity are less selfish than we think. This happened just before Easter; and there was a great deal of extra work to be done to prepare for Easter. There were 21 children making their final preparations for First Reconciliation, with the First Holy Communion Mass in May.

There were also several young people being prepared for Confirmation. During Lent, the parish had a different visual display to illustrate the Readings each Sunday. Without exception, these displays were outstanding, and even the smallest child could make the liturgical connection.

There was a multiplicity of other parish activities going on, including several social events. In all these activities, it was obvious that everyone gave 100%.

I would venture to say that all these activities were useful mechanisms to cope with community grief. But the Big Issue was not altogether resolved. This was bereavement without a death. The people were suffering something they had never experienced before, and their priest was grieving too. That brings us back to the first concern.

As a Church, we have a good record on coping with individual grief; but community grief is a mega problem. We see this again and again when celebrities die suddenly. Princes Diana's death was a powerful example where it took the nation by storm. How can we cope? This parish community was in a state of deep trauma – as if it was bashed around by a huge spiritual tsunami. This was not helped by the fact that there was some hope that the beloved priest might return to them as their spiritual guru. Rumour, counter-rumour and gossip did not help. It was obvious that the community shared a collective pain. I have had lots of experience of sharing pain with individuals and families but seeing a whole community grieving was an altogether different encounter. I was lost on how to deal with this issue and I felt that I needed professional guidance but there was nothing available.

Several times I sought guidance without success.

In the end, I decided to walk with these people as much as possible. As always, with God the darkness of night gave way to morning light. God's people had the answer. The more they threw themselves into being a faith community, the greater a proud and powerful sense of community emerged.

The well-established ministries in the parish came into their own. The Welcoming Ministry were out in the street, so much so that I suggested that one of them should be selling *The Big Issue*. Another parishioner responded, "she is the Big Issue" – reminding me that a sense of humour helps with pain and grief. Everyone was aware that that priest himself was not being offered any meaningful help by the Diocese. There appears to be nothing in place to help a priest who is burned out. There are those who blame the priest himself because he did not tell anyone that he was in crisis. This is a fair comment; but, once he made his condition public, there must be a proactive means whereby he knows that he is loved and cared for, should he be willing to co-operate. There is no such mechanism. I would recommend the creation of a small group of no more than ten lay people, with a few priests or deacons who have a capacity to care for and walk with priests in this situation. They need to respond immediately to a crisis. In all cases, love and spiritual guidance should be offered again and again while the crisis lasts.

In the same way as in a good secular organization, an employee who has a breakdown will be offered support in terms of counselling or even residential care, this is no less than a priest deserves.

When I shared my concerns with a priest friend, he said that when the Body of Christ became an institution, it lost the sense of love and care and that if the institution is cared for, nothing else matters.

Finally, for me, I was the real beneficiary of my

encounter with this community. I experienced great acts of kindness and generosity, so much so that I thought every parish should go without a resident priest for six months every five years. We priests underestimate the enormous contributions the laity makes to parish life. When it came time to leave, I searched around for three words to describe this extraordinary people, in prayer those words became enthusiasm, vibrancy and love, 'and the greatest of these is love'.

The Priest's arrival in a New Parish - Hospitality Makes all the Difference

Arriving in a new parish presents the priest with acute challenges – and even more so for one who has been the proud owner of a Freedom Pass for four years. Rather than taking on new pastures, he should be spending more time in the celestial waiting room like others his age. Instead, I arrived in Christchurch as parish priest in December and have been getting to know the strengths and weaknesses of my new flock; and likewise, the parishioners must get to know my own strengths and weaknesses.

After spending 22 years in my last parish, I took a sabbatical of four months before coming here. The personal, spiritual, and physical benefits were enormous. During most of that time I took my place in the pew, which offered some profound lessons. I asked myself several times if I would want to be a regular worshipper in the community I was visiting if this was the kind of welcome Catholics gave to other Catholics at the Sunday Masses.

In many cases, the priest was not seen before or after the Mass. These experiences had a big impact on me, and it led me to reflect on the importance of hospitality and the difference it can make. For example, the greeting

Catholics who are out of touch with the Church get at the church door may be the first contact they have had since they drifted away. If visitors, strangers and even regulars do not feel welcome, they may never come back again. Consider for a moment those people Jesus welcomed - the great and the good with the sinner, the prostitute, the tax collector and even a Samaritan woman. Some of these people became instant disciples and instant missionaries.

One definition of hospitality is the relationship between the guest and the host; it involves showing respect for one's guests. To the ancient Greeks, hospitality was a right. The host was expected to make sure the needs of guests were met. There is a fundamental truth that some of the people who come to church on a Sunday are in a fragile state, mentally, spiritually and physically. This may be especially true of those who have drifted; but it is also true of people who are experiencing significant losses or challenges in their lives which have shaken their confidence or security.

A warm welcome can make all the difference to these people and, without it, they can be made to feel worse. In my current parish, people receive three welcomes: at the door, from the pulpit before the first hymn and finally from the celebrant. But the kind of hospitality I am talking about involves more than the welcome we give people at Mass. It is about showing respect to those who ring the presbytery bell, including everyone from the delivery man or woman to the lonely elderly person, or the couple who come asking to be married in the parish or for the baptism of their child (whether or not they are married) – and it involves giving children a special welcome.

They are often the chief evangelisers in young families. Making children feel part of the parish family and having a good Liturgy of the Word for Children at the family Mass encourages children to want to come to church. It is also a place where their parents can learn how to pray with them and can be reminded how much God loves us through what their children are hearing.

If, on the other hand, parishioners are intolerant of the noise generated by children, an altogether different message will resound, and you will have no children or young people in the church.

We have wonderful ways of communicating the Good News these days. In his message on the forty-eighth World Communications Day last June, Pope Francis told us that the Church needs to be concerned for, and present in the world of communication, in order to engage in dialogue with people today and to help them encounter Christ. She needs to be a Church at the side of others, capable of accompanying everyone along the way.

The revolution taking place in communications media and in information technologies represents a great and thrilling challenge; and we can respond to that challenge with fresh energy and imagination as we seek to share with others the beauty of God. Pope Francis went on to say that the connections we make through communications media need to grow into true encounters. We cannot live apart, closed in on ourselves. We all need to love and to be loved.

Ask yourself what your church noticeboard communicates – and how your parish uses social media and email. Are your parish newsletters sent out by email? Are they available online and in hard copy? Do you use the local radio, local newspapers and are your services and events advertised on the High Street? These are the places where people can be reached effectively.

There are many people asking the 'big questions of life' – questions like 'Why we are here?' and 'What is the purpose of life?' – and digital communication can be a means of reaching 'to the ends of the earth' (Acts 1:8). During my time of exchanging the pulpit for the pew, I asked myself far too often how good Catholics endure the poor liturgy I had experienced week after week. In my opinion, every deacon, priest and bishop should have this experience of turning the tables. It would help them appreciate the importance of planning a good Sunday liturgy.

This is, of course, especially true of the Easter liturgies of the Triduum when the Church reaches its liturgical climaxes at the Easter Vigil and on the feast of Easter itself. Easter offers many opportunities to invite people to celebrate the risen Christ, God incarnate, who died and rose to free us from sin and death.

It is an opportunity to show ourselves as an 'Easter People' – a people who believe that the Cross transformed all suffering and pain, and the Resurrection secured the promise of eternal life. It is this paschal mystery, this Easter faith, that we are called to live each day. Recall the story of the disciples on the way to Emmaus and have dialogues with the men and women (and children) of today to understand their expectations, doubts and hopes. A hearty welcome is a sure sign that everyone who crosses the threshold is dearly loved by God and his faithful people.

Celibacy

In former times, the gift of celibacy was a sign of the Kingdom and it has served the Church well. It has now become a relic of a former age. Most of my non-Catholic neighbours accept me as a minister of religion, but they have a great difficulty in my non-marital status. Celibacy has no meaning for most Catholics either. There is no reason at all why we cannot have a variety of ministry, with some married priests, some celibate, some part-time, some full-time. The combination of ex-Anglican Clergy who have become Catholic Priests with those who are celibate adds to the richness of ministry in this Diocese and I understand that it works well in other parts too.

Priests Changing Parishes - how to say goodbye - ways to Part.

Change is the one thing in life which is constant. My bishop has asked me to move to a new parish after spending 22 happy years as Parish Priest of Havant and Emsworth. While I agree that a move might well benefit the parish and me, a gentle process of grieving began in the parishioners and in me once the announcement was made. Curiously, the anticipation of absence makes the heart grow fonder; and people began to say noble things about me as if I had died. In fact, it was better than that because I could hear the nice things, they were saying about me. I too began to express appreciation for the parishioners as I began to compliment them on all they do so well.

There is always a grieving process when a priest leaves a parish. Apart from the practical arrangements, with the packing up of his possessions and moving them to the new parish, there are the heart-rending farewells to people with whom he has shared life during the years he has been in the parish. This operates on a spiritual level as well as the emotional. To be able to separate those two spheres helps him enormously to cope. People often take for granted the intensity with which a priest is involved in the lives of individual parishioners. I've always been very aware what a great privilege it is for me to be caught up in the most intimate details of parishioners' stories.

According to the Baptismal Records of the Parish, I have been involved in 479 Baptisms of children, not to mention some adult Baptisms at Easter. There is a great vibrancy and excitement when new parents come to request their child to be baptised. It is a great compliment to be caught up in the dreams and expectations of brand-new parents which often includes the wider family.

Weddings too are the classic high point of a priest's ministry. I have done 118 weddings some of them being roller coaster events. There was the couple who had a passion for string so that the whole Church had string everywhere. Or the couple who wanted to be married in the middle of winter so the building could be festooned with candles---no electricity was used creating a unique atmosphere.

Funerals are great opportunities too. I can only hope that, over the years, I was of some comfort to those who were in pain of grieving. In 22 years, a priest may be involved in several funerals of members of the same family; and every time, the most beautiful stories emerge, to the extent that I have frequently wished I had known more about the deceased while they were still alive.

I was amazed at how my time in Havant touched a mega part of history. The death register began in 1855 when Havant was in Southwark Diocese and this was filled in 2009. In both registers I was involved in the funeral rites of 391 people.

In people's personal struggles, I have often seen my own frailty and vulnerability, but I have always been inspired by their inner spiritual strength. Raw times in parish life are counter-balanced by the high points, and weddings come into this category. We have had some glorious weddings. Then, there is the whole area of reconciliation. Pope Francis recently asked us not to treat the confessional as a torture chamber – but to treat it as a celebration of the day of our baptism. If any priest can leave a parish having made that request a reality, he has served his people well and they him.

But by far, the best in parish life is the rhythm of the liturgical year. Each year I am amazed and grateful to those who contribute with expertise and generosity to the cycle of our spiritual journey. Every event and every year is gloriously different, so long as one does not keep the notes of last year's sermons.

I have come to appreciate that a priest leaves the parish with more than he had when he arrived. I love the respect people have given me regarding my limitations, my gifts and my freedom. I have discovered that the laity is much more gifted in certain areas of parish life than I am. This discovery is a spur to let go of non-priestly activities, however important they might seem to the priest. The days of the priest as the one-man band are truly over. The priest who insists on being the 'jack of all trades' is in denial of the real talents in the community with which he shares his life – and he is denying the laity the opportunity of making their rightful contribution to the community. Stewardship helped me to come to terms with the multiplicity of talents in the people.

Priests are like ships that sail into port, stay a length of time, become engrossed in our faith journey, and then suddenly they have left port with a different cargo. The people are the living stones of the Church, and provide structure, continuity, enthusiasm, faith, love, courage, and a wide range of other virtues which make the presence of Christ very real.

It is a wise bishop who requests his priests to move parishes rather than making rather than making demands on them. A bishop with such wisdom will receive the enthusiastic support of the priests. The bishop can otherwise become an agitator-in-chief, especially if he moves priests for the sake of it or when he tries to place a square peg in a round hole. The latter often happens, much to the detriment of many people. In Australia, the bishop is aided in his decisions about moving priests by an advisory body. This could be a help.

The move reminds me of the time that a priest announced his departure from the parish and two women in the front row started crying. The priest said, "Ladies, ladies it is not that bad.... after all, the bishop has said that he is sending a nice priest". One of the women said,
"The bishop also said that the last time".

The Parish Mission

Over 12 months ago, five Parishes in the Havant area, with great courage, decided to hold a multi-Parish Mission. The Sion Community was invited to conduct the two-week Mission to mark the Year of Faith. We nominated two people from the five parishes to become the preparatory team. The Mission has just finished but our area Mission is truly beginning. The last two weeks have been the most remarkable two weeks in my forty years as a Priest. The response to Havant Pastoral Area Mission has been outstanding in many wonderful ways.

The barometer for the success of the Mission was set high at a very early stage- in fact, on the first Monday of Visiting Week. Only on Christmas Day have I seen so many people in St. Joseph's. I asked myself whether these people could stay the course of a two-week spiritual marathon. How wrong I was! At every event for the whole two weeks there were glorious opportunities to be renewed and refreshed, and to rejoice in what it is to be a Christian in our times.

Even at the times when numbers were smaller, they were very special events. The people of our Pastoral Area surprised me by the way that they rose to the occasion of Mission.

The Scriptures could not have been better chosen to challenge and renew us. The difference between the two weeks could not have been greater because we were drawing one year to a close during the first week, while waiting, hope and expectation exploded in us in the second week of Mission, which was the first week of Advent. Several people have remarked how, through the Mission, they have been blessed with a deeper faith in the Lord.

The commuting between churches and intermingling became a mission as each of us had to think, 'where are we today?'. Because we had to move out of our normal spiritual zone, we were challenged by a bigger church, with new people, in Horndean, Waterlooville, Leigh Park, Hayling Island, Havant and Emsworth. Some were blown away by the beauty of our churches; others were reacquainted with old friends; while others compared notes about their children who went to school together. A wise old sage in one of our parishes said:

'the Holy Spirit is at work among us....'

The final Mass of the Mission was held in Oaklands Catholic Secondary School. The Sunday morning Masses in all the Parishes were suspended, and people were encouraged to join in one celebration. Hundreds of people turned out. We passed on the baton to the school itself by presenting the pupils and the Head with a lighted candle because the school is holding a

Mission in March 2014, also conducted by the Youth Section of the Sion Community.

The power of Touch in Catholic Cultures.

I was very taken with Chris Monaghan's 'Wrestling for a blessing - is there a place for touch in the Church today?'

I was beautifully challenged by this question recently. The Apostleship of the Sea asked me to be Chaplain on the P&O Cruise Ship *Ventura* for Christmas, the New Year and the Feast of the Epiphany.

The Apostleship of the Sea is a charity formed in Glasgow 100 years ago to look after seafarers. It is now a worldwide organization, with a great missionary purpose of looking after those who 'go down to the sea in ships'.

My brief was to minister to the crew, most of whom come from the Philippines, Kerala and Gozo. There are 1,100 crew of all ranks on board the *Ventura* and many of them are Catholics. The reason the Chaplain is on board for so long is that the Feast of St. Stephen, New Year's Day, and especially Epiphany are significant days for these communities.

In the dining room where the crew eat is a Holy Shrine, which contains many different religious objects. It is very noticeable that when the Catholics come to eat, they first reverence the Shrine by bowing, and then they touch different parts of it. It is obvious that the touch itself is a prayer, as it is done with such dedication and reverence. Considering that these lovely people only have Mass a few weeks each year, this prayer of touching is what sustains their faith, empowers their spiritual wellbeing and sustains them on their journey through the

High Seas.

The Parish of the High Seas is like no other on Terra Firma and the ministry of the priest is also quite different. One major difference is touch. On those significant days mentioned above, the crew have Mass at 11:30 p.m. after a full day's work. There are always people on board who call the community together by putting notices everywhere throughout the ship announcing that there will be Mass in the Crew Mess.

There are people who lead the singing, with spirit and devotion. There is never a problem about getting readers. But when it comes to the sign of peace the touch exchanged between them is electric. The Sign of Peace with the priest takes on a new dimension; not only is it firm and genuine, but it is done with a reverential bow of the head as they take your hand to lift it to their forehead. It is a gesture that is deeply spiritual, holy, and natural.

Flexibility is the essence of chaplaincy ministry on a cruise ship because if you miss an opportunity, the occasion may never come again, especially if you are coming to the end of the trip.

This is just one example. As I left the self-service dining room after dinner one evening, the young man whose job was to welcome diners asked me to give him the Sacrament of the Sick. I was surprised because he looked the picture of health and vibrancy. I thought very quickly, and I suggested that we could do it then and there if he could get olive oil from the chef. Immediately he disappeared into the kitchen, which gave me time to think about the order of the ritual of the Sacrament of the Anointing of the Sick. Fortunately, it took the young man longer than expected, so that I was ready when he returned.

At the entrance to the dining room, we confessed our sins, and I recalled as best I could the instructions of St. James. Again, from memory, I recalled the invitation of Jesus to come to him with our heavy burdens and he will refresh us. I invited the young man to accept Jesus as gentle and humble of heart. All the while he held the small container of oil with reverence and great dignity. I laid hands on his head and prayed spontaneously, and then I anointed him, again using the words of the Rite from memory. We said the Our Father, the Hail Mary, and the Glory Be. The young man held my hands with great reverence and again he lowered his forehead in blessing. He thanked me with enthusiasm and returned to the kitchen with the oil before he resumed his ministry of hospitality with the greatest smile I have ever seen. But even in Western Christianity we need to be aware of the crucial part touch plays in our lives.

After Midnight Mass in the Theatre of the *Ventura*, a young couple approached me to request a simple ceremony to commemorate their daughter, who was killed on 27 December 2018.

She was a highly motivated student at one of our great universities when she decided to travel to a foreign country on her own for the Christmas Holidays. Shortly after Christmas Day 2018 somebody suggested that she should go down to the shore to view the enormous waves early in the morning. She did this on 27 December. As she viewed the enormous waves, she turned around briefly, and a freak wave came and took her out to sea, where she was lost. Her family were completely distraught, and the parents had to collect her body and take it back to the UK.

They had come on the cruise in order to be at sea on the first anniversary of her death, to commemorate their loved one. They had in mind to light a lantern and let it waft over the waves created by the *Ventura*. Fortunately, I checked with the Reception Desk who firmly told me that this was highly dangerous and was completely forbidden.

We had to rethink the ritual, and the mother suggested using roses which could be easily scattered over the waves. So, the three of us gathered on the balcony deck over the waves.

The Holy Spirit prompted me to ask the couple about the last year. Out came the most powerful expression of grief I have ever encountered. They spoke in turn about what they had experienced during those 365 days, each day bringing a new aspect of pain, guilt, or remorse. They expressed regrets for allowing their daughter to travel alone. They were distressed that they had not been there to comfort her in the final moments of her life. All the while, they were gentle and calm in their profound sorrow.

As I listened to these remarkable people, I became aware that some of the people sitting round the deck had joined us. Total strangers surrounded us and listened. Eventually I spoke spontaneously about their love for each other, their love for their daughter and their two other children. We placed our hands on each other's heads and I blessed them with generous words. The bystanders joined in the embrace and touched the grieving couple and each other.

Then the wife took a red rose petal and cast it overboard into the waves, and husband and wife did this in turn until all the rose petals were gone. I looked around to see several people in tears. But, more importantly, this young couple released their own personal pain, suffering, sorrow, and grief into the waves of the Atlantic Ocean. This ceremony could only be done at sea and it was emotionally symbolic because this young student had been taken by the sea. If only we observe with keen eyes we are 'being touched by the very life of God'.

(Citation: **GRUFFERTY, T. March 2020.** *The Furrow*)

The Parish of the High Seas

For the last two years, the Apostleship of the Sea has asked me to be the Catholic Chaplain on P&O Cruise ships during the Christmas period. The first cruise was around the North Sea, which was no joke in the middle of a very dark winter. The cruise included a port visit to wonderful cities such as Copenhagen, Oslo, and Amsterdam, but we saw little of these places because it is virtually dark until 10:00 am, and dusk comes in again about 15:30 p.m.

Because of this experience, I resolved never to do another cruise, mainly because it prolonged the dark days of winter for me. My resolution was firm until the Apostleship of the Sea offered me the chaplaincy on the *Britannia* in the Caribbean for Christmas 2018. How could any human turn down such an offer? Not only was the location most attractive but the voyage was for two weeks, covering Christmas and Epiphany.

Equally importantly, I was much better prepared pastorally for the role of Chaplain this time. The guidelines from the Apostleship of the Sea are clear. The chaplain's priority is to the Catholic crew members. Most of the crew are devout Catholics from Southern India and the Philippines. It is clear from the start that these lovely people demonstrate a different spirituality from Western Catholics. They love to touch and kiss the priest's hand as they bow their heads. It is a gesture which calls for a personal blessing and they often do it in public, with no embarrassment. If the priest gives a personal blessing, he receives the most radiant smile in return, which is also a blessing.

Mass for these people is crucially important, but because they are on board ship for anything up to nine months, they are rarely able to participate in the Eucharist. As a Church, we really need to find other ways for people to receive Holy Communion other than at the celebration of Mass itself. I would suggest that twice a year the Chaplain consecrates enough hosts to provide the crew with Holy Communion at a Eucharistic Service every Sunday.

We would have to make many mental adjustments liturgically and would also need to train spiritual leaders on board ship. Given the spiritual strength of many crew members, the potential for on-going formation is enormous.

Many of these people are already powerful missionaries of the Faith to a wide cross section of the passengers. A great number of guests on both cruises remarked on the charm of those who clean the cabins and serve them at table. There is always a warm smile, which I suspect is required by the cruise company but nevertheless, the charm is genuine and powerful.

The other lovely discovery that I made was of the importance of the Prayer Room in the crew quarters. This is a place of prayer and reflection and it is used by many members of the crew, not just the Catholics, though it is created and maintained by the Catholics on board. There are many Catholic images displayed in the Prayer Room.

Catholic memorabilia, such as rosaries, miraculous medals, and holy pictures, are greatly appreciated. The Apostleship of the Sea provides the Chaplain with many of these items and some of them find their way to family members miles from the ship. As soon as these items appear, they are scooped up and treasured like gold dust.

The blessing of Holy Water during the Chaplain's final Mass on board ship is also a special occasion, as many people bless themselves several times each day.

The wider repercussions of being a Chaplain are profoundly significant. For example, Midnight Mass on board ship is a big attraction and is greatly appreciated by everyone on board. This year, we had Midnight Mass in the ship's main theatre. Immediately before Mass there was a concert, which meant that the stage had to be transformed in a short time. Transformed it was, with wonderful Christmas images all over the theatre.

The theatre became a church very quickly. The crew arranged everything, which included Christmas Carols in abundance. I was very keen that, just as many of the crew serve us food at table, so they should serve us spiritual food at the table of the Lord. The spiritual connections were not lost on anyone who attended this special Mass, as it was the most frequently mentioned reaction, in the comments after Mass.

The other great spiritual gathering was the Festival of Lessons and Carols for Christmas Day itself. Anyone on board who had a true sense of Christmas would attend this. On this cruise, the captain and I conducted this service, with crew members doing the readings.

There is also an interdenominational religious service on those Sundays when the ship is at sea. These are conducted by the captain or senior officers.

Life on board ship is a real experience, and you see the entire spectrum of human life displayed before you. An elderly couple are sitting across from me in the best restaurant on the *Britannia*. They have just ordered their first course, with the best Rioja to drink. They lovingly toast each other, then suddenly in walks a much younger man who is the spitting image of the man at the table. Clearly the younger man is seriously disabled, with physical and mental problems. The couple continue with their meal, with their son the centre of their attention, as if everything is normal, which of course for them it is.

The lesson for me was clearly that nothing ever seems as you expect, and sometimes Jesus himself walks into a situation to turn all appearances upside down. Another significant encounter happened when I went to the room where we were allocated to have Mass each evening at 18:00 p.m. for the passengers. In the room was a group of people, and it was obvious that they were Jews, praying as a preparation for the Sabbath. They were wonderfully welcoming. We had a fascinating discussion about what they were doing and what we were about to do. The breaking of bread and the drinking of wine were both at the heart of the two ceremonies. The Jews left the room, and we followed the instructions of Jesus.

When you leave the cruise ship, you leave with the impression that the entire experience is somehow unreal, and yet for thousands of people this is their world and their lives. As the Church in the British Isles we should take great pride that the Apostleship of the Sea does so much to look after seafarers, not just on the luxury liners, but on all ships across the oceans.

This is particularly true since the charity prepares to celebrate its centenary next year. Here is a very brief history of this unique charity with some of the excellent things it provides.

The Apostleship of the Sea

The origins of AOS had several independent beginnings. The first recorded events come from Wimbledon College where volunteers began sending devotional books and magazines to seafarers on 12 ships. They also enrolled seafarers into a prayer association so that they would pray for them and the seafarers could pray for each other. In 1891 the Society of St. Vincent de Paul began visiting people on ships in Bristol, Sunderland, and Tyneside.

It was not until 1920 that the Apostleship of the Sea had its formal foundation in Glasgow. The greatest need in those days was in providing temporary accommodation for seafarers while they were in port. In former times, ships spent days in port, so AOS provided hostels where seafarers could stay. Hundreds of volunteers from local parishes were extremely generous with time and funds in providing for these hostels.

With globalisation, the drive for greater profit margins and technological advances, it soon became clear that time in port was dramatically reduced. Today's seafarer no longer spends days in port but just a few hours. However, the basic human needs of those at sea have not gone away.

As with all good organizations AOS has recalibrated its charity work to provide drop-in centres in the docks and close to where the ships birth. These centres provide e-mail and telephone terminals where the seafarer can contact family and loved ones. An exceptionally large number of those at sea are married with wives and young children in Kerala and the Philippians. Verbal and visual contact is essential as they may not see their families for anything up to twelve months.

I know from experience that following days at sea there is a great blessing to set your feet on solid ground. That is where we humans belong. However enthusiastic we might be to travel, there is no place like home. If those who visit our shores receive a warm welcome with a smile, we have blessed them. We often forget that 95% of those who work on ships are from poor countries. They send all their wages home to provide for their loved ones. Speaking with the crews of the cruise ships, education has a high priority for it enables people to break free from the poverty trap. They are deeply indebted to the West for the opportunity to work, as we should also be indebted to them.

AOS in the Parish/School.

If you want to highlight this charity in your

parish, especially on Sea Sunday, (14 July this year), there is a Parish resource on the web page. If you want a guest speaker contact the Parish Co Ordinator, Salvina Bartholomeusz on 020 7901 1932 or email: **salvina@apostleshipofthesea.org.uk**

There are interesting school resources designed around the national curriculum enabling pupils to learn about shipping, including the life of seafarers. **www.apostleshipofthesea.org.uk/resources -schools**.

The charity has grown, developed and flourished beyond the imagination of its founders 99 years ago. It is now a global network that supports all those at sea, regardless of religion, ethnicity or gender. This care is vital as many of the crew can be away from home and family for anything up to twelve months. When I asked the crew of the Britannia, what was their greatest need, again and again the word 'loneliness' was on everyone's lips. There are port chaplains in many of our busiest ports, like Tilbury, Southampton, Felixstowe, and Aberdeen, but where is no port chaplain, there is an army of lay volunteers in smaller ports.

In certain parts of the world, Apostleship of the Sea is also known as 'Stella Maris' –Our Lady Star of the Sea. This is a beautiful title because it is an ancient title for Our Lady. Just as seafarers depend on the stars so many of them guided and loved by The Star 'Stella Maris'.

Those at sea are modern-day heroes upon whom the prosperity of most of us depend. Without them world trade would cease, and the shelves of our supermarkets would be empty. If you just consider the items you had for breakfast this morning tea, coffee, fruit and the wheat in your bread – all these arrived on these shores by ship. If you drive to work, most parts of your car, the petrol and the oil came here by ship. I live on the edge of the Solent and daily I see oil tankers sail up the Solent to the Fawley Oil Refinery. The Refinery moves 270,000 barrels of oil every day and provides only 1/3 of fuel for the UK. Each tanker with real people on board has enough fuel for every car in the UK for six hours.

These facts prove that the pastoral and spiritual care provided by Stella Maris is on the increase. The Apostleship of the Sea and its cousins have a bright, if challenging, future.

Lest we forget, there are extraordinarily strong ecumenical relations between all the charities that work for seafarers across these islands.

The parish of the High Seas is quite different from the parish of 'terra firma' and the maritime family is constantly in motion. The command of the Lord to 'launch out into the deep'(Luke 5:4) is forever real for many our fellow human beings. The prayer for those who go down to the sea in ships is authentic and beautiful.

(Citation: GRUFFERTY, T. *The Pastoral Review*)

Thanksgiving Prayer for Seafarers

Almighty God, we give thanks for all those who work at sea.

We acknowledge our need for the food and raw materials they transport. We recognise that they are sometimes in danger and their long absences often involve sacrifices in their family life.

Help us to show our gratitude, not only in our words, but also in our actions.

Through Jesus Christ our Lord. Amen

Our Lady, Star of the Sea, Pray for us.

Holy Doors are open doors
End of the Jubilee Year of Mercy 2015

A supply priest in my area was due to celebrate two Sunday morning Masses, but he was taken ill in the early hours of Sunday morning. His wife (he is a convert Anglican clergyman) rang the lay person responsible for that community to say that her husband would not be able to celebrate the Sunday Eucharist.

The lay person concerned showed his mettle, so much so that by the time 196 people turned up for Mass at 9 o'clock, a group of loyal parishioners was there and ready to explain that there would be no Mass, but that the community would gather to pray as usual. Another group of people operated the same procedure two hours later for Mass at 11 a.m. Only one person left to find Mass in a neighbouring parish.

It turned out to be a joyous experience, which was widely discussed. To me, as a priest in a parish nearby, it demonstrates that the laity have grown enormously in their recognition of their baptismal right to exercise the priesthood of the People of God. This is a dramatic change of mindset that would not have been contemplated 40 years ago.

With the New Evangelisation, there is great emphasis on the truth that every baptised person is called to be a disciple. To organise a Liturgy of the Word at the last minute for a vibrant community is exercising one baptismal calling. What impressed me about this community was the experience of a friend who went to worship there that Sunday. Although she really did want Mass, she was astonished at the warm welcome she received and could not resist the invitation to stay. Almost without noticing it, we have moved from being a 'fortress Church' to be a 'pilgrim Church'. Like all pilgrims, we are never sure what is around the next corner. Pilgrims together need one another, and we need the Holy Spirit as a route map to guide us towards the final destination. A pilgrim Church looks outwards with courage, confidence and hope. A fortress Church is locked up and inward-looking, while a pilgrim Church is very much the opposite, open and outward-looking. A pilgrim people are less concerned with who is sharing the adventure, but profoundly aware that they are sharing the faith.

As pilgrims, we need to encourage everyone to become new evangelisers. We need to train everyone how to be a Catholic outside the narrow confines of the parish church. We are frequently fearful of Christianity out in the High Street. Admittedly, many of the structures and props we have come to rely on have already disappeared, or are rapidly disappearing, and we seem to be paralysed when it comes to replacing them with new methods. As a pilgrim people, we need to recalibrate our approach to a wide range of issues. Every Sunday provides a unique opportunity to show who we are and the richness we have to offer.

Those who cross our threshold for anything, a liturgy or otherwise, will come for a multiplicity of reasons. Some will have deep spiritual needs, some will have faith, but many will have no faith at all. They will sit in the pew because they love the person sitting beside them, or because Granny from Krakow would wish them to be in church for this occasion. There are countless different reasons why people turn out for church.

Let those of us who are there every Sunday not disappoint them, but welcome them with love, and with hope. If every practising Catholic determined to make a difference to all those who share the sacred space, we would have huge spiritual revival across the nation. Priests and people need to put on a welcoming smile, but a smiling community is only the start of a daring endeavour. I was really taken with Leonard Cohen who died recently. As the name suggests he was Jewish and very proud of his Jewish roots. However, a huge influence in his life was the nanny who cared for him as a small boy. She was a Catholic and she read New Testament stories to him. Those stories, and especially the story of the Resurrection, had a big impact on Cohen's other dark outlook on life.

If returning Catholics who come to Mass find hope and love, we have communicated the real meaning of the Incarnation. If people leave Mass knowing that they have received somebody special, that they have encountered a loving Saviour, the year ahead promises so much more for them.

To illustrate my point, I have often told this little story from the time of the autocratic rule of Nicolae Ceausescu in Romania in the 1970s and 1980s. Some American volunteers worked in an orphanage in Romania.

When it came to Christmas, they told the Christmas story and then they asked the children to draw what they had heard. When they came to look at the drawings, they found that one child, called Misha, had two babies in the manger.

They asked him if he had understood the story, and he replied that he understood the story perfectly. He told them that when he came to place the baby Jesus in the manger, Jesus asked him if he had a Mama and a Papa. When Misha said he had nobody who cared for him, Jesus invited him to stay with him. 'When I got into the manger with Jesus, he said he could stay with him forever'. Then he began to cry because at last Misha had found somebody who was not going to hurt him but would love him forever.

If our people can leave Mass with the same certainty as Misha, we will have succeeded in a superb mission. We have just closed the Holy Door of Mercy at the end of a special year of Jubilee. But a Year of Mercy is far too short because we need the generosity of God's forgiveness every day and every year.

In John 10:7-10, Jesus says: 'Very truly, I tell you, I am the gate for the sheep. All who came before me are thieves and bandits; but the sheep did not listen to them. I am the gate. whoever enters by me will be saved, and I will come in and go out and find pasture. The thief comes only to steal and destroy. I came that they may have life and have it abundantly.'

I wish we could take the lock and the hinges off the Holy Door and leave them off forever. Jesus as the gateway is open to us as much today as he was last year, and he will remain open without condemnation or disapproval.

(Citation: GRUFFERTY, T. December 2016 *The Tablet*)

Alpha in the Catholic Parish Context

I have been doing the Alpha Course in the Catholic context for many years. At first, we operated out of the presbytery sitting room, with members of the group leading summaries of talks by Sandy Millar, the vicar of Holy Trinity, Brompton, and his then curate, Nicky Gumbel. The presbytery kitchen became the Great Havant Bake Off as two people took responsibility for the food each week. The food in those days was always fun. We made every effort not to be too elaborate, sometimes without much success. Then a small revolution took place as we discovered we could view the talks on VHS.

This made life much easier and the discussions afterwards took a lofty turn for the better. With the current presentations on DVD, yet another revolution has taken place, in that they have become films with a marvellous interaction between people of all ages.

The presentations are a joy to watch, highly professional and always challenging to those with or without faith. Alpha in the Catholic context takes the same shape as all Alpha courses.

Each meeting is a combination of a meal, which often is a huge icebreaker, followed by the film and a discussion in small groups. It is a 10-week course, which sounds a long time, but the weeks fly by. There is also an important awayday or weekend, which should not be omitted under any circumstances. The fundamental Alpha logo is a question mark, with the crucial question: 'Is there more to life than this?' We have just finished our most recent Alpha course. This was done with the great difference that it was aimed at those already in the pew.

The initiative came from Richard Martin, whom we appointed as a part-time, paid lay formation director 18 months ago. Initially he collected a team of 25 people from across our pastoral area of six parishes. It was fascinating to watch how the team bonded because, at first, not everybody knew other members of the team. The bonding process consisted of a mini-Alpha course of three sessions called 'a taster'. It soon became apparent that this team was bonding well together under the direction of its leader. Catholics in the pew were then invited to a one-evening taster, without commitment.

Even at this stage, we discovered that many people had some prior experience of Alpha. As a result of the taster, 60 people signed up. Fortunately, we had already decided to use every inch of space of the parish property, including the whole church, even the sacristy. As it turned out it was the best use of any parish property in my experience.

We used the parish centre for the meal and the main church for the presentations. Preparation of food for 85 people presented a huge problem. All parishioners across the pastoral area were asked to sponsor the supper, even if they were not attending the course. The response was outstanding. One person gave a cheque for £600. Those who attended were asked to contribute as well.

For the actual provision of food, we approached a catering friend, who supplied a menu with great variety. We had an excellent team who served the food, and cleared up afterwards during the presentations, so that the parish centre was ready for the group discussions.

Outcomes from the Alpha Course were fascinating. Through a questionnaire, we discovered that, of those already attending church, 77 per cent made new friends, 57 per cent had their faith strengthened, 46 per cent were open to a personal relationship with Jesus, and 43 per cent found greater peace in the faith. Other aspects of the survey were equally encouraging. There is nothing else like it in parish life; in fact, I doubt if there is any other course or initiative that could generate such positive results in three months. It would be interesting to ask the same questions in 12 months' time. We held the recommended celebration evening to evaluate the experience. About 20 people spoke about what they had gained from the course. Without exception, there was positive feedback from those who spoke, including five exceptional testimonies of how Alpha had given a new direction to their spiritual well-being.

One lady had a phone call from her son, who asked what she was doing on that night. She said she was rushing to Alpha. 'But Mum, I thought Alpha was for those who wanted to become Christian?' She went on to elaborate how she had become a better Christian during the course even though she is a cradle Catholic. Another lady spoke about how she had had no faith when she started the course, but a new light had been turned on for her, even if she is still uncertain about what comes next.

For me personally, it was a really enriching experience to go round many of the groups and to discover that each one dealt with the topic under discussion in a different way. But what fascinated me most of all was the emergence of lay leaders, who were growing in their passion for the Good News, for Jesus, for others in the community, for the world and for life. It was obvious that people were growing in confidence. Many participants had become aware that there was indeed 'more to life than this'.

The Alpha Course does wonders for those who wholeheartedly engage with it. It enables people to attain or renew a relationship with Jesus. It brings the Gospels alive and it touches the basic tenets of the Christian faith. It brings an evangelical dynamism to Catholicism and it also introduces new prayer methods. It deepens the Kingdom of God in people. Nobody would claim that it deals specifically with Catholic teaching, with ecclesiology or with the seven sacraments, and this is not its purpose. There is a good variety of presentations specifically on the Catholic faith (none more professional than "Sycamore" with Fr Stephen Wang; go to **https://sycamore.fm**).

Despite the absence of specifically Catholic teaching, I think that every bishop, including the Bishop of Rome, and every ordained minister of the Catholic Church should do the Alpha Course, so that we rediscover what it is to be a believer in Jesus. It has a remarkable ability and success in forming disciples. I think that it should be part of the preparation of young people for Confirmation and I would also recommend it, at least in part, for parents requesting Baptism for their children.

Priesthood
Promotion of Vocations of the Priesthood

Our Diocesan Vocation's Director is also a full-time parish priest. While he does his best to promote Vocations to the Priesthood, the profession is featured once a year on Good Shepherd Sunday. There is a loose association of all the Vocation Directors in England and Wales. Otherwise, there is nothing professional on the recruitment of new priests. Priesthood as a career is never mentioned in our Catholic Schools. Priests themselves are the best promoters of the profession, but how many actively encourage young men to think about the priesthood?

For this article, I asked several priest friends if they encouraged their parishioners in the direction of the priesthood. Not one was enthusiastic about the promotion of vocations to the priesthood. I must emphasise that all of these are considered good priests and are in good standing with their bishops.

The vocation to be a priest is a fascinating and a noble calling, but many priests have lost the sparkle to shine. The whole Church in England and Wales needs to establish a professional team with a clear mandate to recruit students to the Priesthood.

Seminary Training in Parish Life - Me and My Shadow

I have lived alone in a lovely Presbytery for 20 years and I have my own routine and my own way of doing things. I am happy to be with people, but also happy to close my front door and be alone. So, when our Diocesan Vocations Director asked me to have a seminarian in the parish for nine months, I had the greatest of reservations.

For one thing, the thought of somebody else sharing my space was daunting, and I wondered how I would cope with the responsibility and the company of an extended pastoral placement. Priestly formation should not take place in isolation from the People of God or within the confines of the seminary; this is something of which I am convinced. After speaking with a few friends, consulting parishioners and some of the priests in our pastoral area, I agreed to the request.

On his first Sunday with us, I invited the seminarian to introduce himself at all Masses and he was given a warm welcome by the parishioners. People were curious about life in the seminary; he found that lay people wanted to know what the students do in a seminary for six long years. There seems to be a fascination about what life is like in monasteries and convents – and about how men are prepared for the priesthood.

The parishioners' curiosity prompted me to learn more too. I began by logging on to the web pages for Allen Hall in London and for St John's, Wonersh, where our student is studying. I discovered in both seminaries that the word 'formation' has replaced the expression 'studying for the priesthood' – a profoundly significant change from my time in the seminary.

The modern-day seminarian receives human, spiritual, intellectual and pastoral formation. Of course, the ultimate formation for any of us must be in Christ himself – and being formed in the likeness of Christ is a significant move for any human being. Human formation helps the student to learn the importance of relating well to others; they learn to be open, friendly and, above all, they learn the importance of service.

Their spiritual formation includes the development of a sound prayer life – both private and public. This includes daily Mass, the Divine Office and spiritual direction. Their intellectual formation includes learning theology (where they study Christology and the Trinity, the sacraments, liturgy, ethics and Scripture studies). Their pastoral formation puts the student at the coalface, interacting with parishioners and learning how to respond to their needs. The pastoral placement is like a finishing school. With this brief understanding of where the seminarian was coming from, we set about compiling a pastoral plan that would give the student the widest and most varied experience possible, one that would help him put the theories of what he is learning into practice.

These pastoral placements are a formidable challenge for a parish community; but they are also exciting. In former times, students put theory and practice together in their own time, if at all. I know several contemporaries who, after many years of priesthood, have never integrated the two. The Martha and Mary in us must always be brought together; the contemplative must marry the pastorally active priest in parish life.

Keeping that balance and retaining both in equal measure in ministry will help our seminarians become good priests. Relationship is at the core of ministry, so getting to know parishioners is crucial.

Our student is being invited to everything – all meetings, coffee mornings, jumble sales and car boot sales, clergy meetings, *Churches Together* meetings and much more. Two other local priests will welcome him for one month each. This will widen his experience and give him a flavour of the bigger Church. No aspect of parish life is excluded. Our student will visit the sick and housebound in the parish and he will visit our local prison. The Catholic chaplain of Queen Alexandra Hospital in Portsmouth has invited him to join the hospital chaplaincy team during his stay and he will spend Fridays doing the rounds with the visiting team. Our student will also spend at least one day a week in the local Catholic primary school – where he will gain experience of sharing the faith with children – and once a month he will write a reflection for the newsletter.

During his stay in the parish, the Anglican priest and the United Reformed minister have agreed to let him shadow them for one Sunday each. The priest is seen to be a person with authority, and it is imperative for seminarians to understand what this means.

The word 'authority' comes from the Latin verb *augeo* and it can also be traced to the Greek verb *auxano*. which means 'to grow", 'to increase'. It carries a similar, corollary politico-cultural significance, as in, 'to promote'. People in authority, thus, are people who grow, who increase in understanding, in skills, etc. and they are people who promote others. This is what a good leader does; and good leadership is vital in the Church.

Our example of how authority can be used, what kind of leadership model we should be following, comes from Christ, who empowered others during his time on earth; the one who continues to empower all of us through our baptism when we are anointed priests, prophets and kings. The lived experience of the parish community has a vital influence on the spirituality of the priest. His formation goes on every day and in every situation in which he finds himself, long after he has left the seminary. The ongoing formation of the laity is also a lifelong task. The spirituality of the community relies on this; its spirituality is only as good as the leader's spirituality and the leader's spirituality is only as good as the spirituality of the community. It is beginning to dawn on our parishioners that this pastoral placement could be a very enriching experience if they allow themselves to be formed too.

I hope it will be an opportunity for us all to discover and develop our understanding of the priesthood of the laity as well as the ordained ministry.

Figure 6: "The London Virgin in Prayer"
by Giovanni Sassoferrato

The Power of Prayer

(I was inspired to write this letter to a fictious mother as a result of listening to a real mother on a National Express bus from Heathrow to Gosport. She loves her son so much that she assumed she had 100% control over him, even his job in Lloyds Bank. I had hoped that she would have finished her story before I got off the bus, but that was not the case. Therefore, I have created the end for her!)

Dear Mum and Dad,

I know that you will find this very distressing. I have decided to give up my very good job in the bank, despite the positive promotion I received in March. You have often praised me for the prospects the bank had for me. I will not be coming home tonight because of the arguments that this will cause.

I have found Jesus and joined the Catholic Church. This happened some time ago, but I was not able to tell you, for obvious reasons. A few months ago, Mum, you remarked how consistent I was on doing a cycle run on Sunday morning, but the truth is that I was at Mass down in St. Joseph's. I know that you will not believe this but everybody in the Parish is very friendly and welcoming. They are so enthusiastic and genuinely like my company, as I do theirs. I have never experienced such a sense of belonging, even greater than that wonderful family holiday we had in Whitehaven two years ago, as I do in the Church.

I thought that I might write this letter in two parts because there are other surprises to come as well, but I opted to tell you everything now. You see I have such a great love for Jesus and the people in the Parish that I have asked to join the priesthood. I have been accepted for training which will take six years. I will be going to the Seminary in September this year.

Now, Mum, I know what you are thinking, but I could easily join an enclosed community of monks and you would hardly ever see me again. Yes, Dad, I know that this decision will grieve you greatly.

You have often spoken of how you look forward to your grandchildren bearing the family name. That may now never happen unless the Catholic Church changes its rules on clerical celibacy.

I realise that this is going to be a powerful shock

to you both. That is why I left a bottle of Rioja and a bunch of red roses in the garage, but before you open the wine, finish reading this first, because there is more, and another surprise.

I am sure you remember the day all three of us visited the National Gallery in London as a treat for my 8th birthday. All three of us stood in silence before Giovanni Sassoferrato's painting of 'The Virgin in Prayer'. For me it was a great mystery but none more so than what soaked into my very being that day. You remember you had to drag me away even though I knew you had arranged other exciting things for the rest of my birthday.

The painting has inspired me for the last 16 years so much so that I have secretly visited the painting many times since. It is serene, and I found serenity in the person it depicts. It is a profound picture of love, like the love you have both shown me for the last 24 years. Your love has contributed largely to all the decisions I am now writing about. Thanks for taking me to the Gallery all those years ago. Do not blame yourselves for what you did because the consequences are bright and beyond what could ever be expected.

Now, get those roses and open the wine. Don't worry about me. I am staying with very dear friends from St. Joseph's for a week, and next Friday, I will return to that special love only you both have for me. By that time, you will have recovered, and I will have told my friends at the bank that my future investments are already taken care of.

With great love and the deepest affection.

Your loving son,

Brian

(Citation: GRUFFERTY, T. February 2019.
Catholic South West)

A New Understanding of Priesthood

In our glorious past, the Church has responded powerfully to the needs of the day. When there was a need for reform in the Church, the religious orders responded in a miraculous process. When there was a need for hospitals or education, the Church spearheaded the response.

Now with priests we need multiple initiatives. We can have part-time priests. The Anglicans have non-stipendiary priests and some of these are doing wonderful work. We could easily have more specialised ministry where lay people could conduct baptisms and funerals. It is essential to explore a new theology of ministry ordained and non-ordained. Special ministers of the Eucharist are a great example. The sick and the housebound have never had it so good in the Church. When I was ordained, they received communion on the first Friday of each month, today they have Holy Communion once a week and our special ministers are generous in many other ways, far beyond the call of duty.

Clericalism

Submitted to the Tablet in 2019 but not published.

Pope Francis has often spoken of clericalism in the Church. Having been a cleric for 46 years, I set out to de-clericalize myself. For the last few years, I have discovered that clericalism is the greatest challenge of our time. Without noticing it has created an elite in which one group of people think and act as if they are better than others.

Therefore, Pope Francis suggests that it may have caused numerous cases of sexual abuse across the world. It certainly became a strong feature of the ecclesiastical self-preservation which followed. Protecting the clerics, regardless of the crimes, has reached the highest ranks in the Church and is still going on. Timothy Radcliffe says that what really matters is discovering the priority of being brothers and sisters; those are the only titles that matter - not 'Father', 'Very Rev.', 'Your Eminence' or even 'Your Holiness'. But clericalism starts with me, and I wanted to know what my place in the Church was in 2019.

The Pope asked me to strip myself of everything that separates me from the missionary mandate of the Gospel. So here goes. This became a self-examination in the certain hope that I might become a better priest. I wanted to discover afresh something I already knew only too well. What is my real identity as an evangelist, a missionary, a holy man, leader of people, a priest of the Catholic Church in 2019?

For a long time, I have wanted to walk and identify with people as their equal. With the laity we clerics share something in common. That is Baptism. What follows is one personal clerical detox. My first port of call was the name I was given in baptism. 'Thomas' was the name I was given and although I have changed it to 'Tom', I have enjoyed it for 74 years. This designation by name is what I share with all baptised people. I am not certain which Thomas I was named after, but I like to think it was Doubting Thomas. The Doubting Thomas is led into a powerful profession of faith in Jesus. 'My Lord and my God'. Of course, Thomas puts his finger into the Lord's side to scientifically experience the humanity of Christ, but this leads him to the great act of Faith in the Divinity of Jesus. You cannot make a greater act of Faith than 'My Lord and my God' (John 20:28).

With such faith, have decided to drop the title 'Father' and just be called Tom. With my Christian name I can walk with all those others who are called by the name of their Baptism. With them and my Patron I can share their doubts and their certainties, their hopes and fears.

Daniel O'Leary speaks powerfully about the real priests and priestesses in the home. Only in the family can one parent be called 'Father'.

Without a shadow of a doubt, I received my priesthood from my mother who ran a small country shop. She was an untrained midwife and she prepared neighbours when they died for burial. In those three areas she exercised priesthood in a lovely fashion.

She exercised baptism in delivering the new-born; she exercised the Eucharist in selling and often giving away bread and she anointed people in despatching them into eternity. Seamus Heaney used to say that the landscape is itself sacramental.

Without knowing it, we are priests, and we exercise priesthood unknowingly. If Karl Rahner was around today, he might well speak of the anonymous priests who work out the Baptismal priesthood. It is astonishing that we have called clerics 'Father' for centuries despite these words in Matthew 23:9 'Call no one on earth your Father....'

The second thing I addressed was the clothes I wear, especially those garments that separate me from my fellow human beings. For many years I have noticed how people cross over the road when they see a cleric approach and then there are those people who look at you but pretend, they are not looking.

I have not worn the 'Roman Collar' for 25 years and I can honestly say that I am not any less a priest. I am surprised that we have allowed the Roman Collar to become known as the 'Dog Collar' which we have adapted from the Anglican Community.

In allowing these words to be used, I wonder if the bishops of the day knowingly encouraged the term so that their clergy would be on a leash?

As well as the dog collar there are other clerical garments that need urgent attention. The evangelist in lace surplice or in the rich soutane speaks of differences and simply alienates people. The other method of de-clericalization I have personally addressed is to allow lay people to be themselves. For the last ten years of pastoral ministry, I have tried to hold people together, which is not as easy as it sounds. The best way is to be non-judgemental, to praise and encourage, but especially, to listen. Listening to all laity is healing, is forgiving, but above all, allows them to grow in faith. If people know we are listening, they accept with deep gratitude the compassion and forgiveness. Listening without judgement in the confessional is a special blessing for both people engaged in the sacrament.

I really was uplifted when Pope Francis, during his visit to the Capuchin Centre in Dublin, praised Brother Kevin Crowley for feeding 800 people every day without asking any questions. The Pope dropped his prepared text and went on to say that the Church asks too many questions of people including in the confessional.

The mercy of God is far more important than the number of times I had a steak on Friday night. Many people leave the Church and never return because nobody is really listening; no one is encouraging them, least of all the priest. I think that, in walking with the laity, we rediscover the road map.

I have been supplying in various parishes these last few years and wherever the cleric walks with the laity, there is an extra dimension in that community which demonstrates itself with enthusiasm, love, compassion, and, most of all, a missionary zeal.

It goes without saying that if a community is happy and together, outsiders will want to join and, in turn, they will enrich the life of the parish. Donald Cozzens sums it up like this: 'the Priest exercises ministry and receives ministry, he is both pastor and parishioner, a preacher of the word and a listener of the Word, a leader of the community and a member of the community. He is a Saint and a Sinner....". In my self-de-clericalization I discovered that I am a priest not because I am a saint but because I am a sinner. I will always treasure the fundamental truth that if the priest looks after his people, they will look after him.

The Ramblings of a Parish Priest

I am incredibly grateful to a friend for introducing me to *The Furrow* a few years ago. Each edition contains something special. I have before me the six copies from 2011 and I want to revisit some of the important issues therein. The six copies have a wide range of issues and are very rich in meaning and content.

We sometimes need to revisit topics that we might have overlooked or missed. It is like a good racehorse. If she is racing in top form, she thrives on a second or several outings.

This was personally brought home to me recently. I read Pope Benedict's *Jesus of Nazareth* in preparation for Holy Week this year, but in my keenness to get a good homily for Good Friday, I completely missed an important distinction the Pope makes between the Narrative Tradition and the Confessional Tradition in the early Church (pp.248-265).

Then, weeks later in an article in *The Tablet,* Elena Curti pointed out the distinction, with special reference to the ordination of women. I carefully read those pages again and the Confessional Tradition arises out of a juridical structure whereby only men can appear in Jewish courts. That is how Peter and the other Apostles operated.

Running parallel with the authoritarian structure was the Narrative Tradition in which women and very few men are at the forefront of ministry. At the foot of the

Cross, women are noticeable by their presence and even more prominent immediately following the resurrection. Then, nearly all women fade from view.

The Pope has already surprised the entire Church with the Personal Ordinariate of Our Lady of Walsingham, whereby in a short time we have married Catholic priests. Is it possible that there is another surprise, whereby the Pope gives the Narrative Church its head and we have women once more spearheading ordained ministry in the Church? I am certain how some members of the Ordinariate would react.

As you can see, I will not confine my ramblings to *The Furrow*, but this publication will remain the springboard of the rummage.

In February, Mary Redmond reminded us that there are three *magisteria* in the Church- the Pope and bishops, the theologians, and the people in the pew. It is fascinating that John Henry Newman valued all three equally. Using the Omega process, Mary went on to explain what happened when the Pastoral Council sought a mandate at Mass from the people in the pew. Proper analysis of the results is crucial to any survey, but equally important is action arising out of the ideas put forward from the pews.

A similar exercise is happening in the Diocese of Down and Connor called the 'Listening Process' (*Intercom* June 2011). Almost 100 meetings have taken place across the diocese, but again and again, there is a call to action. It is indeed heartening that lay people have been involved from the outset. The experience is described as greatly encouraging and stimulating the faith of those involved. Parishes, schools and universities are engaged in the process. Emerging from the exercise is a strong need for catechesis in faith formation, a desire to be involved with a commitment for clergy and laity to work in collaboration. It is hoped that a Pastoral Plan for the Diocese will grow out of this listening venture.

A similar exercise is going on the Diocese of Kerry. Activities like this are sure signs that the Church is willing to move on and into new waters, perhaps even to the extent that the laity become the *magisterium* of the Church in the 21st century. It is certain that the Bishops and the Doctors have not served Mother Church very well in recent years. The age of the laity might well have come, based on the firm foundations of the Second Vatican Council.

Gerard O'Hanlon very cleverly wrote about a National Consultation. He spares the feelings of nobody when he describes the Church as dominated by clericalism that is secretive, defensive and excessively deferential. Those words alone are enough to ponder and pray about, especially for every priest and bishop. We might well pray about them in the sacristy before we begin the main Sunday Mass.

Gerard calls for a National Assembly to renew the institution, which might in turn renew the person as the two go together. He even suggests a National Synod without the bishops. Dare one add that the individual needs renewal while the institution needs a revolution?

The sad thing about this article is that the call on the whole Church to come together has fallen on deaf ears. A single voice crying in the wilderness takes a long time to be heard.

With a great urgency, Paul Prior called on us to throw open the doors of the upper room. Not only are we locked in fear, but we have placed ourselves in straitjackets of ideologies, habits, mindsets, paranoia, pessimism and even ritual. I would like to add the current stress to manage everyday ministry which is increasingly piled on these days.

Paul suggests that we have locked ourselves in the Tabernacle with Jesus where he is safe, but most importantly of all, we are safe. Even if we tried, we cannot break free. And yet we can set the downtrodden free, to open new doors and break new ground.

I am very taken with Donal Dorr's reflections on the appointment of bishops. Once a bishop is ordained, he remains a bishop for the rest of his life, and usually in the same diocese. The Bishop assumes the status of a prince of the Church with stately titles and dress. We call them 'My Lord' and cardinals 'Your Eminence'.

By contrast, the religious superior is elected for 6 years and he/she is elected for one more period of office if they have done a good job. This is a much healthier approach to leadership and accountability. Instead, it is seen as promotion, whereas the **election** of the bishop should be seen as one of service. Donal says that there is urgency for priests and bishops to radically change the way authority is exercised in the church. He gives suggestions on how to move forward and without necessarily involving Rome. These six points cannot be overstated enough:

1.   Parishes   in   clusters   must   work collaboratively. In our Diocese we are five years down the road in our Pastoral Plan and already priests and laity are working together for the local church. We have a long way to go but the collective responsibility is emerging in the most surprising places and people.
2.   Abandon the terms 'Parish Priest' and, 'Curate' and work together in teams with lay people. No one priest can be good at everything, but most are good at something.
3.   Many influential Catholics are hurt by the child abuse scandals and how this issue has subsequently been handled. There is the additional grievance that the Vatican is doing everything to block the spirit of the

Second Vatican Council. Renewal cannot take place until these issues are addressed, aired and action taken. The listening process in Down and Connor and elsewhere might well be the right catalyst for this reconciliation to take place.

4.   Once people have ventilated their hurt and anger, they will begin to play their active part in the life of the Church.

5.   Donal's final suggestion is based on the opening remarks of his excellent article, that many pillars of society have been thrown down - bankers, politicians, bishops and priests. Now the last thing we want is for these leaders to make any attempt to climb back up again. They must walk humbly with their people, as some are already doing with great courage, they must work together in teams. Bishops should ask to relinquish responsibility after ten years and return to the ranks. There are plenty of precedents for this, including the famous Archbishop Tom Roberts who handed over the Archdiocese of Bombay to his auxiliary in order to become a chaplain in an oil tanker travelling round the world. Subsequently he played a significant part at the Second Vatican Council.

6.   I think of all the material published in the last six months 'Restoring Credibility' needs the widest circulation because the writer sets out to ask, 'What's possible?' not 'What's wrong?' Seamus Lillis Page 21.

The Church of Today

51 years ago, Vatican Council II emphasised the crucial importance of lay people in the Church. The *Degree on the Apostolate of Lay People* says that the Church cannot survive without the laity. For the last five decades, we have tinkered around with a high level of fear and procrastination on doing something about the laity in Parish life.

At the same time, the laity themselves have been more and more exposed to golden opportunities to live out their Christian mission in the wider world, most of all in their places of work. 'Go forth, the Mass is ended' is lived out powerfully and successfully across the land. These leading lights are the real missionaries of our time as they exercise Ministry and Word to their colleagues and friends.

I have read again the Decree on the Laity, only to discover a rich resource for dynamic team ministry. Right at the start the degree says: 'In the Church there is a diversity of ministry but unity in mission' (Chapter 1 para 2). Even after 50 years, we have hardly begun to digest the diversity, mainly because we have confined ourselves to a narrow view of mission.

We still think that the mission of Christ is the sole preserve of the ordained. And this continues even though we call every person baptised 'a Priest, a Prophet and a King'. Lay people are rarely given the opportunity to exercise their priestly role, not to mention their prophetic ministry in the Church.

Add to this the thoughts of Pope Francis. He says that clericalism is the greatest distortion of the Church. He says that the clock has stopped for the phrase 'it's time for the laity', due to a great desire among the ordained to hold on to control, regardless of the consequences. The Pope reminds us that every ordained person was originally a lay person. Closing parishes without consultation because there are no priests to celebrate the Eucharist is rampaging clericalism. It is also a serious denial of all the baptised. This is a dictatorial denial of the ministry of lay people and their mission in the Church.

The questions that need to be asked of every ordained person daily is: 'Does my ministry block? and 'What is the Spirit saying to the Churches?' (Rev 2:29). The truth everybody needs to realise in the parish is that the person with the real mission is the one with a genuine relationship with Jesus.

These are the people who have the diversity in mission mentioned so frequently by the Council Documents. Thank God we have numerous such people in our parishes. Priests and bishops need to take account of the numerous people who are doing great work for the Lord.

When I arrived in my new Parish 18 months ago, I set out to recognise, acknowledge and affirm such people. It is not an easy task, but one that needs to be done. It is like an informal parish audit to ascertain the strengths and weaknesses of a community. I deliberately took a different approach to my priesthood.

I set out to be radically different to the way I operated for the previous forty years. I was determined not to be a control freak, to observe carefully what was happening in this community, to say 'yes' to everything and everyone, and to make no major decisions whatsoever and never without as wide a consultation as possible.

The process was helped by the fact that the community had been without a resident priest while I had taken a sabbatical for three months prior to arrival.

For me personally, the initiative was liberating because it was instigating a teamwork approach to parish life. For some people in the parish there was confusion because here was a different kind of priest, while for the majority this was a great opportunity to continue their ministry. Some quickly realised that the days of 'Father knows best' were taking a different direction. It was fascinating to watch people grow in confidence as I tried to affirm and encourage them. The process is ongoing and throws up many surprises.

I have to say that from the very first day there were things I wish I could have changed, but I resisted the clericalism for at least a year. The informal audit paid huge dividends. It quickly dawned on me that what was happening in this community needed 'grow-more' in a professional way.

I made a new discovery that my job as priest is to enrich these people with Good News and empower them to share their faith in all the circumstances of their lives. Briefly, my mission was to enable everyone in the parish to exercise to the full what they were commissioned to be in Baptism. There is still some resistance around that expresses itself as: 'Father should be doing this...'

For the first time in many years, my ministry was energised. But if this was to really take place, I needed help in training and formation. I discovered a parishioner who was working with a group of parishes 20 miles away. I heard great reports about Richard Martin who was responsible for lay formation. The Holy Spirit was involved too because Richard was coming to the end of a three-year contact.

Without a shadow of a doubt, he was the one to draw on the gifts of the people and push them into a dynamic Church. We have now employed him 25 hours a week to work across six parishes with a diversity of needs. Already, there a clear sign that people are flourishing in ministry. He has established a series of networks for a wide variety of ministries so that the weaknesses in one community are enhanced by the strengths in another. Networking has a huge benefit in that it comes naturally to people and all one must do is get them together.

I look forward to the people of all these communities taking ownership of a Church that is diverse but united in mission.

(Citation: GRUFFERTY, T. August 2016. *The Tablet*)

The Priesthood in Transition

I have carefully monitored all correspondence on ministerial priesthood in the pages of the Catholic Press for several years now. I would venture to suggest that the current ministry, and therefore leadership in parish life, is in a very dark place. Numerous reasons are suggested why this might well be the case, not least of which is clerical sexual abuse and the subsequent fall-off in numbers entering seminaries.

In many ways, we have entered the dark ages of the celibate priesthood. Most of us are blind to the fact that we are in transition of one mode of ministry to another. The Fortress Church is becoming the Pilgrim Church in which everyone, clerical and lay, move along the path of life on an equal footing. In this great epic journey, we can easily identify with our spiritual predecessors who walked the same path, sometimes with food or without food. Christopher Lamb reminds us that Pope Francis frequently says that the Church that walks together stays together. Walking together means taking care of our fellow pilgrims. I think we have many people in ministry who need basic care, especially from those who have the means to provide it.

At the same time, Lay leadership in Parishes needs approval and affirmation. The Parish of Our Lady of the Assumption, Doncaster has had three lengthy periods from 20 months to 7 years in the last 23 years in which the laity conduct funerals and do loads of other things. I love the mantra of this community. 'Gratitude for the past, enthusiasm for the present and hope for the future'. Would that every parish, those with or without resident priests, had the same passion!

Personally, in the last six years when I encouraged lay people to exercise the priesthood of the People of God, they did so with expertise and enthusiasm.

A Reflection on the Parish Priest.

I am not sure where I found this but there is some truth in it and in the different versions of it.

If he visits his people, he is nosey.

If he does not visit, he's a snob and lazy.

If he preaches more than 10 minutes, it is too long.

If his sermon is less than 10 minutes, he cannot have prepared it.

If he runs a posh car, he is worldly.

If he does not drive, he is always late for appointments.

If he tells a joke at Mass, he is flippant.

If he does not tell stories he is far too serious.

If he starts Mass on time his watch must be fast.

If he starts late, he keeps the congregation waiting.

If he takes a holiday, he is never in the parish.

If he does not, he is a stick in the mud.

If he runs a Parish Bazaar or any social events, he is money mad.

If he does not, there is no social life in the parish.

If he has the church decorated, he is extravagant.

If he does not, the church is shabby.

If he is young, he is inexperienced.

If he is getting old, he ought to retire.

But when he dies or leaves the Parish, 'there has never been anybody like him'.

Retirement of Priests

Every Diocese needs a small group of dedicated people to care for the priests in retirement. When we did a small survey among our retired priests a few years ago, we discovered that the majority were happy with their ministry. There are phases of retirement; some wish to contribute by helping, without the responsibility, while others wish to be fully retired. We active priests need to be aware that we should not take advantage of those who are willing to help.

Into this category, I place those priests who are in trouble, including those who have been wrongly accused. The Church has a serious moral responsibility to endeavour to ensure that justice is done in every case and, where false accusations are made, wrongs are righted with immediate effect. The Nolan Report solved several problems for certain people but created a barrage of legal and moral difficulties for others. We should not be too surprised that nobody wants to join an organization with so many loose ends.

In conclusion, these are a few thoughts about modern day ministry, and they are intended to provoke discussion and comment in this Year of the Priest. Those who have the power to influence the future development of ministry must provide the means whereby the Eucharist remains central to what it means to be Catholic in the 21st century.

Reflections

Two American Tourists were in Rome when they saw a beautiful telephone. They asked a local what it was for. He said: 'It is a direct line to Heaven, and it cost 1000 Euro.' They decided that this must be a tourist scam. They saw the same phone in Berlin, in Paris and in London, except in London the price of the call was £10.

When they went to Mass in Dublin, they found the same phone in the church and it said: 'Direct Line to Heaven -only two Euro'. They said to the priest: 'We have been all over Europe and we have seen this phone, with outrageous prices for a direct call to Heaven but here it costs only 2 Euro...how come? The priest said: **'But from here Heaven is always a local call!'**

Catholic Squirrels

Three churches in Havant had a serious problem with squirrels. Each church was overrun with troublesome greys. One day, the Methodists called a meeting to decide what to do about the squirrels. After much prayer and consideration, they determined that the squirrels were predestined to be there, and they should not interfere with God's divine will. The Anglicans got together and decided that they were not able to harm any of God's creations. So, they humanely trapped the squirrels and set them free a few miles outside of town. Three days later, the squirrels were back. It was only the St. Joseph's Catholic Church who were able to come up with the best and most effective solution. They baptised the squirrels and registered them as members of the Church. Now they only see them at Christmas and Easter.

When I was working for Stella Maris recently on the Cruise Ship *Ventura* I was walking along the gangway when I met a well-dressed couple returning to their cabin for the night. She said: 'Fred there's a vicar. I am not sure if that is a good or a bad sign'. To which I replied, 'Have a great night's sleep'.

The clergy of our Diocese were challenged recently to consider if we were Caretakers, Undertakers and Risk Takers. An altar server was overheard to say,

'I lost my missile last Sunday'.

A Letter in the Tablet April 2010

At the Rite of Election last Saturday, Bishop Crispian Hollis elected catechumens to be baptised and confirmed at the Easter Vigil and he also elected candidates to be received into full communion with the Catholic Church at Easter. I am certain that this was repeated in every cathedral in the country.

Among the people I saw at the ceremony were young and old, families and single people, including many from ethnic backgrounds. It is always inspiring to see such numbers wishing to join the Church at the Easter Vigil. They want to join the Church for the right reasons, and many are enthralled by the new faith they have found. To experience the Rite of Election is to see a bright future for the Church. This runs contrary to the common view from the pews and some of our pulpits. There is a doomed fatalism about the future of institutional religion in certain quarters. We blame the media for the bad press we receive as Christians, but the media people have caught the disease of pessimism from the Church itself, a pessimism that is highly contagious. There is always a danger that insiders can cause more damage than outsiders.

Because of these new Catholics, we need to turn this malignant attitude on its head. We really need to harness the enthusiasm and the new-found faith of those we shall receive into the Church this year. We need to become aware that there are more people out there who are searching for truth, hope and faith. Dare I say that we need to go in search of them.

In these new Catholics, an energy needs to be released so that it soaks into the very soul of what it means to be a Catholic in 2010. There is an optimism that must be tapped into otherwise we sell the Good News short.

Carrot, Egg and Coffee

A carrot, an egg, and a cup of coffee. You will never look at a cup of coffee the same way again.

A young woman went to her mother and told her about her life and how things were so hard for her. She did not know how she was going to make it and wanted to give up. She was tired of fighting and struggling. It seemed as one problem was solved, a new one arose.

Her mother took her to the kitchen. She filled three pots with water and placed them on the burners on a high setting. Soon the pots came to boil. In the first, she placed carrots; in the second she placed eggs, and in the last one she placed ground coffee beans. She let them sit and boil, without saying a word. In about twenty minutes she turned off the burners. She fished the carrots out and placed them in a bowl. She pulled the eggs out and placed them in a bowl. Then she ladled the coffee out and placed it in a bowl. Turning to her daughter, she asked: 'Tell me what you see'. 'Carrots, eggs, and coffee, she replied.

Her mother brought her closer and asked her to feel the carrots. She did and noted that they were soft. The mother then asked the daughter to take an egg and break it. After pulling off the shell, she observed the hardboiled egg. Finally, the mother asked the daughter to sip the coffee. The daughter smiled as she savoured its rich taste and aroma. The daughter then asked, 'What does it mean, mother?'

Her mother explained that each of these objects had faced the same adversity: boiling water. Each reacted differently. The carrot went in strong, hard, and unrelenting. However, after being subjected to the boiling water, it softened and became weak.

The egg had been fragile. Its thin outer shell had protected its liquid interior, but after sitting through the boiling water, its inside became hardened. The ground coffee beans were unique, however. After they were in the boiling water, they had changed the water. 'Which are you?' she asked her daughter. 'When adversity knocks on your door, how do you respond? Are you a carrot, an egg or a coffee bean?'

Think of this: Which am I? Am I the carrot that seems strong, but with pain and adversity do I wilt and become soft and lose my strength?

Am I the egg that starts with a malleable heart, but changes with the heat? Did I have a fluid spirit, but after a death, a breakup, a financial hardship or some other trial, have I become hardened and stiff? Does my shell look the same, but on the inside am I bitter and tough with a stiff spirit and hardened heart?

Or am I like the coffee bean? The bean changes the hot water, the very circumstance that brings the pain. When the water gets hot, it releases the fragrance and flavour. If you are like the bean, when things are at their worst, you get better and change the situation around you. When the hour is the darkest and trials are their greatest do you elevate yourself to another level? How do you handle adversity? Are you a carrot, an egg, or a coffee bean?

As James Mallon says in his 2019 book *Unlocking Your Parish*: 'When a Parish engages in pastoral activity it needs to ask itself if it's trying to catch fish (Evangelisation) or feed sheep (Discipleship) because fish don't eat grass and sheep don't eat worms' (p.31).

The Visit of Pope Francis to Ireland - World Family

I am amazed at the wholesale negativity surrounding the visit of Pope Francis to Ireland. I would like to boast in a positive way on five things that inspired me.

As the cavalcade transferring Pope Francis from Dublin Airport to Aras an Uachtarain, the aerial views of Dublin were outstanding in the morning sunshine. Considering the millions of people watching, those pictures did more for Irish tourism than any other event in our history. The eyes of the world were on Ireland for 36 hours. Down the road the nation will reap the benefits.

The address of the Taoiseach, Leo Varadkar, was an outstanding tribute to Catholicism, especially since Independence, with an open invitation to every Irish citizen to enter a new spring of acknowledgement and cooperation. Catholics of all walks of life should reply positively to the bold address. All Catholics need to act on the Taoiseach's invitation to bring justice and healing to all the victims and survivors of abuse in all its forms in the Church and society.

The compassionate manner of Pope Francis towards children was a profound statement on how everyone should treat children and young people. This was evident throughout the trip, but especially on his arrival at Knock Airport.

The Pope's unscripted remarks to Brother Kevin in the Capuchin Day Centre were a clear signal to me that the days of Spanish Inquisition have ended in the Catholic Church. A less judgmental Church means a place in the pew for everyone, all inclusive, regardless of gender, race or creed. As Pope Francis said in his address to bishops on 26 August 2018: 'Do not repeat the attitudes of aloofness and clericalism that at times in your history have given the real image of an authoritarian, harsh and autocratic Church'.

The fifth observation belongs to the people who ventured out to meet the Pope. We should not underestimate the fellowship and love of most of those who took part. I was with 40 thousand sunshine people in the rain at Knock. What took place between us will stay with me for the rest of my life. The joyful encounter was helped enormously by the stewards, volunteers, the Gardai and all those who organised the wonderful occasion.

I think we should build up rather than tear down, embrace rather than alienate, include rather than exclude for that is what Jesus does. Everyone in Ireland and the Irish abroad should hold their heads high because of what took place last weekend.

Under the heading 'a spiritually of care, consolation and incentive', Pope Francis says that 'the family has always been the nearest hospital'. On another occasion he said that the Parish should be like a field hospital ready to receive the sick and the wounded.

Both metaphors challenge the daylights out of modern-day parish life, taking the family and the parish as the extended family together.

It is only in recent centuries that the care of the sick became the responsibility of the hospital. Prior to that, most people who were unwell were cared for by their loved ones. Even to this day, in some parts of Africa, the family unit has joined forces with the Hospital in providing food for the patient. In a recent survey in the USA, it was revealed that there was better health outcomes and a quicker recovery in those patients where they family were engaged in their treatment.
(BMJ Publishing Group Ltd)

Jesus in the Street

Our Pastoral Area, consisting of six parishes, had a 'Welcome Home' campaign for Christmas 2015. Reports of larger numbers at Mass were most encouraging across all six communities. One person who received a personal invitation remarked that for the first time she met Jesus in the church car park.

. For all our Masses we had planted our most gifted people to welcome others in the car park. All of them used their charismatic charm in welcoming everybody into the car park, especially visitors and newcomers.

The idea of Jesus in the Car Park is an interesting one. When you take account of the public life of Jesus, most of it was done outside, and only a fraction of his ministry took place in the Temple or the synagogue. The entire Passion narrative takes place outside and, even today, the Stations of the Cross on the Via Dolorosa are outside, and it is only when you come to the Holy Sepulchre that the Passion moves indoors.

I maintain that we have lost that important and crucial aspect of the Life of Jesus in our time. The Mediterranean countries are much better at meeting the Lord in public places. People are at ease with Jesus in the Street. 'The Misteri de Trapani' in Italy is one of the oldest Street Plays of the Passion in Europe.

It has been performed each year since Easter 1612 and lasts for anything from 16-24 hours. Such street plays and processions were once common across Catholic Europe, the 'Semana Santa' in Seville in Spain being perhaps the most famous. These are major liturgical events attracting large numbers of participants.

I was in Tenerife for the Feast of the Epiphany this year and the arrival of the Wise Men in the Harbour of Los Christos is a real outdoor spectacle with the Wise Men on camels. Large crowds followed them to the town centre to enjoy street theatre.

Great credit for re-enacting the life of Jesus outdoors must be given to Peter and Ann Huntley of the Wintershall Estate. Since 1995, over a quarter of a million people have followed Jesus and his Disciples around their estate near Guildford. The events and experiences of those participants are well documented. In recent years, their charitable trust has taken this further, performing parts of the Passion in Trafalgar Square in London. I was involved in the early days of planning Havant Passion Play of 2014 and I am very aware of all the effort these outdoor events necessitate. There is a wonderful charitable trust willing to help Passion Plays in particular- The Passion Trust.

Jesus cannot be locked in the tabernacle nor confined to our churches. On Ash Wednesday this year a group of us in the parish took a daring initiative. We decided to distribute Blessed Ashes to the general public for two hours after the Parish Mass on Ash Wednesday morning. We received a most encouraging response from the public. In the two hours, over 35 people agreed to receive the ashes. Those who received the ashes ranged from churchgoers of all denominations, to lapsed Catholics and atheists.

One woman was very complimentary to us for having the courage to publicly witness to being Christian. She claimed that, while this is still a Christian country, there are too few public demonstrations of the Christian Faith. One man, when asked if he would like to receive ashes said: 'No thanks. We lost the Ashes last year to Australia!' The initiative gave us an opportunity to pray with three people who were suffering from major bereavements in their lives, which suggests that there is a great need for a prayer ministry in public places. I was blown away by how quickly people poured out their troubles.

One of the most rewarding aspects of the

experience was how the 12 people who took part in the exercise worked together and found their natural role either in talking to people, giving them leaflets or distributing blessed ashes. Some parishioners came to meet us out of curiosity. Another surprising result was the subsequent interest from parishioners who were not there; they were astonished at some of the questions which we had been asked.

The venture was not all plain sailing, as we did receive some outright refusals, which emphasised the importance of having the support of the group.

The net result was that we took a risk as Jesus often did. The parish that does not take risks with the Good News needs re-appraisal. This was a risk that worked in spectacular fashion because the Holy Spirit was clearly with us. There was a great sense of prayerful solidarity in the 12 people who took part from the Parish. On a sunny Ash Wednesday morning we encountered the young and the old, the friendly and the hostile, the committed and the indifferent, the loquacious and the silent, all of whom are God's People for certain. I personally took great consolation in meeting people who were totally unchurched and did not know what Ash Wednesday was about.

We should pay extensive tribute to *Street Pastors* and *Street Angels*. These are the light of Jesus in the darkest parts of our towns and cities. While their main task is not to evangelise, their driving force comes from the Lord. They befriend people in night-time venues and offer practical help. *Street Angels* pray with people. It is a known fact that where these organizations operate, night crime drops significantly.

Another place where Jesus can be found is in the halls and outbuildings and warehouses where over 500 food banks in the UK operate.

If we are alert to meeting Jesus in the great world

outside our churches, we will find him in the most unexpected people and places. The Incarnation means he is taking part in everything. Jesus is in the Street more than we think.

Every Year is a Year of Mercy 2015-2016

There will be a great deal of discussion about the closure of the Jubilee year of Mercy on 20 November as the Holy Doors will be closed until there is another year of grace. I hope that, while we physically close the Holy Door, we spiritually open up new doors to mercy and forgiveness. The Year of Mercy is far too short because we need mercy every year and every day. There are many people in the pews every Sunday who need to be convinced that they have received mercy, and that does not take account of millions who left the Church because we were mean with the gift of mercy. In opening those new doors, we need to be liberal, generous, and extravagant with God's gift of mercy. Once the Door of Mercy was opened on 8 December 2015 it cannot be closed ever again. We are already well into The Year of the Priest and I have yet to see any serious theological or pastoral discussion on the present state of Priesthood in the Catholic Church. From the intake of new students who began training for the priesthood this year, it appears that there is a sizable increase. How can we as Church keep the momentum going and motivate those who might be called to serve God in the Priesthood and the Religious Life?

In the last few years in the Diocese of Portsmouth, we have discussed the Centrality of the Eucharist at the request of Bishop Crispian Hollis. As you might expect we have reached the conclusion easily that the Mass is essential for what it means to be a Catholic. Yet many Eucharistic Communities have already faced the reality that they have no priest to provide the Eucharist. How long will these communities be able to remain 'Eucharistic'?

This is happening right across the western world. We need to provide priests so that the Eucharist can remain central. There are several issues, which need to be highlighted in order to drive this new energy.

Emergency Telephone Numbers

These are more effective than dialing 000.

❖ When you are sad, phone John 14

❖ When you have sinned, phone Psalm 51

❖ When you are facing danger, phone Psalm 91

❖ When people have failed you, phone Psalm 27

❖ When it feels as though God is far from you,

phone Psalm 139

Christian Symbols in Public Places

Recently I was traveling on the 18.24 p.m. train from Waterloo to Havant, and the woman sitting beside me was using a tablet computer. It caught my attention when I realised that the woman was praying Evening Prayer from the breviary. When it was clear that she had finished, we talked about prayer in public places. She introduced me to the powerful reminder of the love of the crucified Lord for us. She then went on to highlight the following opportunities available to display our beliefs in a public place.

A bowl of sand reminds us that we are in the desert with the Lord in all the temptations of the modern age.

Placing a candle on the dinner table can be a great sign that we share in the light of Christ. This could be linked to the paschal candle in church at the Easter Vigil and beyond. Parishes can encourage families to have their own Easter candle at home.

The greatest symbol must be the Bible, open and on display, for all to see that we are.

The Knights of St. Columba have wonderful posters for Christmas and Easter but how many are displayed on our front windows?

Churches with open doors are a welcome sign.

A candle in the window for Christmas (Be aware of safety)

The Celtic Background - Family & School Echoes

Replenishing the Celtic Souls from Rich Resources – A Visit to my Native Land

Every time I visit Ireland these days I visit more as a stranger rather than Mac na hÉireann. This is particularly true in my relationship with the Celtic Church. I sometimes feel that I am a stranger looking in rather than a priest of the people of God. In a strange way this is good because I consider myself a pilgrim in search of my ancestral roots within a deep spiritual resource from which I was hewn. With this quest I can replenish the spiritual stocks from the deep resources which can only be found in Ireland. To really find the riches, one must go beyond normal parish life, I am sorry to say. That is not to say that these treasures cannot be found in some faith communities throughout Ireland, but I have yet to find them.

You can easily discover that extra magnitude of the Celtic spirit in places like Lough Derg which I have 'done' several times, or in Ballintubber Abbey or in Knock. This year I searched Croagh Patrick. Ireland's Holy Mountain is an ancient place for the Celtic soul in my native Mayo. It is especially iconic for me because, from where I lived, it was clearly visible on a clear day. The Reek rises 764m above the Atlantic seaboard as a beacon of welcome and challenge.

No other mountain cries out to be conquered, not even Mt. Sinai or Mt. Tabor! Reek Sunday this year became 'Reek Week' in that Mass was celebrated every day during the week leading up to "Garland Sunday'. Each day there was a blend of tourists and pilgrims.

In the little village of Murrisk, the locals know the difference between tourists and pilgrims. Tourists moan about the climb, while pilgrims praise their God about the rugged beauty of the mountain and Clew Bay. Some pilgrims are even shoeless.

In addition, the pilgrim is on an epic journey as a participant in life and as an observer. The climb itself is life in microcosm which only takes three hours, two up and one down, for those who are physically fit. Nobody puts more effort into the mountain than the gentle Mayo man selling "sticks for the Reek" outside Campbell's Pub at the bottom. He told me he cuts the sticks in Galway six months before 'Reek Week' so that they are well seasoned. He is in the renting business too, in that you can hire a stick.

So, with a Galway Zimmer frame one begins the journey. Immediately you become aware that there are several psychological, even spiritual barriers, warning you why you should not climb this mountain. Your age is against the climb and, even on a hot day, the devil puts the thought in your mind that the weather may not last. These barriers are breached again and again, helped by the Patron Saint, and by those millions who have climbed this mountain before you and by those who will continue to do so in generations yet to come. The last leg of the climb demands stamina as it becomes the greatest challenge. Determination pays off as you reach the summit. On a clear day, the views of Clew Bay with all its islands are just stunning.

As one enjoys the views you become deeply aware that you have conquered something within your inner self. This awareness is like Moses standing on the threshold of the Promised Land and being told by God to stand firm, not to be afraid and to be strong. What a magnificent mantra for every day we get up!

I hope that the 20,000 people who climb Croagh Patrick on Garland Sunday have a similar spiritual feeling. I notice that Archbishop Michael Neary, Archbishop of

Tuam and the Apostolic Nuncio, Archbishop Charles Brown also climbed this year. A few more clergy in Ireland need to don their funny hats and 'walk the walk' with their people. After what the Church has been through, I find it extraordinary that priests do not welcome people to Mass and bid them farewell at the end of Mass. Only in two places did I find any interaction between priests and people before and after Mass.

The Prior of the Dominican Church in Athy was very prominent in his Dominican habit as he greeted people as they arrived at Mass. The new Bishop of Kerry also greeted people as they left the Cathedral on the Sunday after his ordination as Bishop. The most profound feeling whilst climbing The Reek is in acknowledgment that all are equal - some might walk faster but climb everybody must.

That equality is crucial for the modern day Catholic, regardless of rank or position. This is also true in the monastic life. In many ways, my visit to Glenstall Abbey was the highlight of my Celtic Pilgrimage. There were 25 lay people present for Vespers - some were young people. I was not enamoured of the colour scheme of the Abbey Church (blues and greens should never be seen!) but what followed was a rich reward.

A solitary monk appeared; he lit the candles on the altar and lit set fire to an incense burner in front of the altar. Then slowly a procession of 15 monks appeared, led by their abbot. The congregation allowed itself to be led into the most exquisite combination of music, singing and smell. Even though we had the words in front of us, nobody actively took part, and yet, everybody was engaged in the *Prayer of the Church*. We were 100% engrossed in the experience.

As I looked around, some were in deep contemplation while others were visually involved. This was the essence of 'full participation' in the liturgy, even though we never said a word or sang a note. The Reading from Vespers echoed around the Abbey Church. The smell and the prayer of that evening followed me around Ireland for the rest of my holiday. It proves what good liturgy can do and its power.

Cashel School Centenary Mass 2010

Sermon for the Centenary Mass of Cashel National School Friday 6th August 2010

What a daft place to build a school! It also involved building a bridge across the little stream outside. Yet the stream becomes symbolic of us all. It flows we do not know where, perhaps into the great wide Atlantic Ocean. The Atlantic is the second biggest of the five great oceans of the world. It takes in 76 million square miles and covers everything from the North Pole down to the South Atlantic. It runs down the East Coast of Canada, America and South America and the West Coast of Europe and Africa, including most of the waterways of Europe. It is great to think that our little stream outside this building enriches the waterways of the world.

Like the stream, when all of us graduated from this exalted academy we call Cashel School, we went to the four winds. Many stayed here and did very well for themselves. Some went, never to return and some only come back for an occasion like this. Like the Atlantic, we went to the four corners of the earth and we enriched the culture and the society we joined.

We should not underestimate the enormous contribution we have made to the world. We might have had a lowly start by comparison to others, but we were grounded in the skills to survive. Some had great adventures and I am always thrilled when I hear how people got on in Vancouver or Philadelphia or Sydney.

I know now why we had to learn by heart the

Rivers of Ireland so that we could navigate our way in the great River of Life. The education we received in these hallowed walls was so designed that we spent the rest of our lives educating ourselves. If I might say so, we did better than anyone expected.

As Mark Twain said: 'I never allowed my schooling to interfere with my education'.

If Billy Swords, Mrs Egan and Mrs Rowley were to meet us in 2010, they would be proud of our achievements. Our parents would certainly be amazed at the progress. Those who built this academy of learning would say that they did a good job in 1910- it was a good investment. We should remember that 100 years ago, Ireland had not yet emerged from being a colony of an imperial power. Building a school here was a bold and a daring venture for Victorian Ireland.

So, I thank you for what you have given to life. For the good you have retained from your days here in Cashel School. The last few days have been a blessing for me as I listen to story after story. Life is a great story and our biography is forever etched in the walls of this school, perhaps on a desk or two. Pat Kneafsey, God rest his lively soul, had learned to write his name before he came to school, and he left his signature on five desks the first day, and that was before he ran away at lunch time. The blessing that St. Paul gave to the Ephesians is the same blessing that our parents and teachers gave to us. They gave us the Power of Spirit for our inner selves to grow strong. It was up to us to do with that whatever we pleased.

They planted love in our hearts so that we could have the strength to grasp the breadth and the length, the height and depth to be filled with the utter fullness of God. It was up to each one to do with that whatever we were capable of doing with that profound gift. This is just one example of that meaningful love.

When I did the funeral of somebody recently in

England who attended this school, the family brought water from Knock and soil from Curryane so that he might be laid to rest with some comforts from home. It was a lovely and moving gesture showing the power of the Spirit working in us. Those special gestures are treasured in our lives and in the schoolhouse, no matter if Billy Swords did block all the heat from my father's turf I have often thought about my days in this school. There are two special places when I have special thoughts about this place.

One is when I am home and I drive past this schoolhouse with all the mod-cons of the modern car, and I count my blessings. The other was a few years ago when I was up on an Inca Trail in the Andes and we were invited to visit a school much more impoverished than the building behind me. I had a profound sense of my blessings, my background, my family, and my school friends and even my teachers. God rest them and all those who have died who shared this academic place of learning.

Pupils of Cashel School mid 1950's

Delia Gallagher R.I.P.

In 1995 I did a Parish swap with Fr. Des Magennis for a whole year. He came to Havant and I went to his parish. east of Melbourne. It was a great pastoral experience for both of us and, we both think, for our respective communities. For one thing, when I returned to Hampshire, I was surprised to discover that Des had handed over many parish responsibilities that I thought were the preserve of the priest. A remarkable learning curve, but it also gave me the opportunity to travel and explore Australia. I did this in style, and one of my best journeys was to visit a family relative in Adelaide. Delia Gallagher was my first cousin. Our mothers were sisters, with her mother being the eldest and my mother as the youngest in the family of 8. Anne Forkan was born in Midfield, the daughter of Andy and Bridget Forkan, (Tunney from Curryane).

Anne Forkan married Patrick Gallagher from Cloonlara and they had 8 children. However, with the birth of her last child Anne died in 1942, leaving Pat with a young family. Suspecting that she was going to die, Anne asked her sister-in-law, Ellen Horkan, to look after the youngest child, Bernie. Ellen survived Anne only by one year. Kate and Ned Horkan took on the care of Bernie and this magnificent gesture has never been forgotten by the family.

With a young family in the home of Pat, this meant the older children had to care for the younger ones. Delia, who as the second eldest, was sent to work in the Swinford Electric and Steam Laundry which was run by the Sisters of Mercy.

After four years, Delia decided to emigrate to London, where she intended to train as a nurse. Sister Benignus, who was one of the senior nuns in the Laundry gave her the name of a contact she knew in London. On arrival in London, the contact mentioned that the best income came from people working as silver-service waiters. Delia opted for the local information because she wanted to send as much money home to the family. She fell in love with London. Eventually she met and fell in love with Tom Tunney from Curnageltha, Co. Mayo. They had three children, Theresa, Kevin and Anne.

In 1968 the family of five migrated to Australia on the £10 scheme. The family sailed on the *Fairsky* from Southampton, via the Canary Islands and Cape Town, as the Suez Canal was closed. As the ship was not built for rough waters, the journey of five and half weeks was horrendous. The one highlight was their views of Cape Town.

When they arrived in Melbourne, they then had to catch the overnight train to Adelaide. The train broke down three times and took 17 hours. But the horrors were far from over, as the family was billeted in Pennington migrant hostel. Tom did not find it easy to get work, but apparently, he was warned about the difficulties by friends before he left London.

Eventually, they found their own accommodation. Another child was born in 1970. Kathleen Fiona became the only Australian in the family. This was followed by the long illness of Delia. The loss of her income plunged the family into serious poverty, which cast a pall of hopelessness over everyone.

While Delia's illness lasted, as often happens, family history repeats itself, because it became Theresa's turn to look after her siblings, especially Kathleen. Thanks to great resistance, prayer and blessings Delia was restored to full health as a much-loved mother, and financial provider. Delia worked in catering and in house-keeping all her life.

Slowly, life improved and the foreign land became home as a place to be loved, esteemed and respected.

Delia and Theresa never forgot their original roots. They have been back to Swinford several times until Delia died in 2011. There is a strange paradox in the offspring of emigrants that, in returning to their roots they discover who they are in greater depth and in understanding themselves.

You see them return to their current home with new enthusiasm, with even a new spirituality. The other observation I have is that, when we are young, we do not always ask the important questions about our family history – 'Why does that branch of the family not talk to this branch?' It is time to build bridges and bring about reconciliation, especially when the real reasons for estrangement are long forgotten.

Theresa contacted me in 2019 saying that she would like to revisit Swinford and rekindle her connections with the vicinity. She invited me to introduce her to members of the extended family and especially, to see where her ancestors came from. We had two glorious days with Teresa, her daughter Marguerite, and her husband. We explored where her grandparents came from in Midfield and in Curryane. The present owner of her grandparent's property gave us freedom to explore the house and the grounds where Delia was born.

Theresa was interested in looking for the spring find it. We visited Colmore school where her mother received her early education.

Cemeteries are a great source of information, so we spent a great deal of time in Kilconduf and Midfield Cemeteries where we found the graves of her grandparents and great grandparents. In the two days, I discovered that Theresa was keen to know something about the laundry run by the Sisters of Mercy in Swinford.

The laundry has long since gone and been replaced with a secondary school for the area. We visited the parish church and the Cemetery where the nuns are buried.

As a result of our search, we contacted Sister Ethna McCarthy who lives in the town. She turned out to be a family relative. She was full of information on the biggest employer in Swinford up to the 1970s when the Laundry closed its doors.

The Sisters of Mercy came to Swinford in 1855 and very quickly they started primary and secondary schools for girls. The Laundry started in 1925. Its main purpose was to provide employment for local people. This Laundry was quite different to the Magdalene Laundries around the country. For one thing, there were no boarders. The workers lived at home and came into work each day. By all accounts, the regime was strict and well organised.

The most famous nun was Benignus, as she had established contacts in cities across the world. So, when her employees told her that they wanted to move on, she was able to put them in contact with her contacts. Delia Gallagher wanted to move to London and Sister pulled out all the stops to establish a contact for her.

In our time, we call this introduction 'networking". In the 50's and 60's this was networking in its infancy, but no less crucial for the welfare survival of all emigrants, especially those leaving the rural West. When I left Swinford in 1964, I realised immediately the importance of knowing the right people who had knowledge of the local scene. We have no idea of the enormous good Sister Benignus did.for those young people leaving her laundry for Manchester, London, New York or Sydney with the name and address of a contact. The career prospects and the potential of the young person flourished because of that kind gesture. It would be great to hear the stories of those who made it good in foreign countries.

It is the people you meet in life that make the journey worthwhile - from disaster to success.

Humble Beginnings - The Forkan Brothers

This story concerns a couple who left the Midfield-Swinford area well before World War II. James Forkan was the son of Andy Forkan and Bridget Tunney. He was born in Midfield, one of several children. Mary Reilly came from the neighbouring village of Tullinahoo. Both families have many current family members and relations in the vicinity.

James and Mary were in England before World War II. In fact, the family returned to live in the Swinford area for security reasons during the war. In the late 40's the family returned to England and James resumed his career in the building and civil engineering industry, while Mary brought up their five children. In the 60's James went into the retail business and was very successful.

Our story concerns Kevin who was the youngest of this lovely couple. He too had a business acumen, but also a free-spirit approach to life. He met and married a lady called Sandra, who also had no fear of doing things outside the normal. They were deeply in love and well matched for each other.

By 2001 they had six children from six years upwards. In that year, both parents decided to take their four youngest children on a trip of a lifetime. They decided to explore Asia and its rich culture. Having sold their home in Purley in Surrey, all six set out for the open road, minus the two eldest children.

They spent the first year in India and they enjoyed its vibrant way of life. From there they moved to Sri Lanka. They spent Christmas 2004 in a small fishing village called Weligama. They had a special Christmas lunch in the nearby Neptune Resort.

Then their way of life was to dramatically change forever. On the morning of Boxing Day, the huge tsunami struck the coastline causing havoc in its path. The family woke up to screams, as huge waves destroyed everything in their path. There was panic as everybody tried to escape the destruction. It was the survival of the fittest as all four children clung to what remained stable. The family saw the sink torn from the wall and furniture turned into matchsticks.

Both parents were missing, as well as Rosie the youngest. Eventually, the survivors began to emerge dazed and traumatised. There were dead people everywhere. After many hours, Paul and Bob found Rosie who had a deep gash on her arm with muscle exposed. She was in a deep state of shock as she said there was no pain.

They gathered in a mosque where they met a German woman whom they had known in the hotel. All four children watched her eat a Toblerone while they were starving for at least nine hours. The children never forgot the scene, but worst was to come. The children never saw their parents again.

The story on how these orphans made their way to the nearest Airport, 200 kms away is a heroic story. The journey took two whole days. Here they were taken care of by the British Embassy. In due course, they were flown back to the UK where there was an emotional reunion with Marie and Jo, the two eldest girls. Marie, who was 22 years at the time put her wedding and her job in pharmaceuticals on hold as she and Liam took her four siblings into their home in Farnborough in Hampshire.

Three months later the bodies of their parents were found. The entire family and friends were able to say their farewells in a highly emotional funeral service in Hampshire.

As often happens, out of great tragedy comes a profound ability to make a difference. And this story is no different.

Bob and Paul wanted to make a difference. They

put their experience of travel to work by creating a new kind of durable flip-flop. In 2012 they launched a brand-new business called *Gandys*. The idea of casual beachwear grew out of the boys' experience in Asia, Australia and America. Immediately the brand was acknowledged by famous people, including Richard Branson, who wears the flip flops in his private retreat in the Caribbean. But that is not all. Profits from the business support orphans all over Asia. The charity is called *Orphans for Orphans*. As a result of their extraordinary success, the brothers have being recognised by Queen Elizabeth and Princes William and Harry. You have guessed correctly; the boys wore flip flops on all the royal occasions.

The two young men have been recently acknowledged as Exceptional Young Leaders and they have been to Buckingham Palace.

So, from very humble beginnings, just outside Swinford emerges a brand with international recognition. We never know what surprises future generations can achieve. I know for a fact that two lovely people from Midfield would be very proud of the name 'Forkan'.

Tsunami Kids—*Our Journey from Survival to Success*" by Bob and Paul Forkan (Michael O'Mara Books) at £16.99 is out now. A percentage of the profits will support the Gandys Foundation.

The Echoes turned into Epilogue.

I am making final preparations for the completion of this book during self-isolation as a result of the Coronavirus, also known as COVID-19 during Spring 2020. St. Corona was martyred in the year AD170. because she interfered in the public persecution of a young man called Victor. Both Corona and Victor are now honoured in the Basilica in Anzu in Northern Italy and are mentioned in the Roman Martyrology.

Most of the echoes of this publication are inspiring and have contributed to a positive outlook on priesthood and on my ministry generally in the Catholic Church in the United Kingdom and in Ireland. But the widespread invasion of Corona has created unprecedented echoes of negativity in the lives of everyone in the world. For one thing, this has created fear and suspicion around the world.

These are different echoes, not heard since the Black Death. Despite the magnificent methods of communication with advanced technology, many people are transmitting, but not receiving. But God has had this problem since Adam and Eve. Even with self-isolation I have become more involved in social media and therein found healthy echoes the likes of which have inspired me. For the last few weeks this has become my favourite prayer:

Lord, help me

Be prepared, but not anxious,

Be aware, but not desperate,

Be vigilant, but not in fear,

Be joyful, but not clueless,

Be faithful, but not careless,

Lord be my hope and strength.

Words from Pope Francis: 'Before falling asleep tonight think about when you return to the streets. When we hug again, when all the shopping together will seem like a party. Let us think about when the coffees will return to the bar, the small talk, when we can stand close to each other once more. We think about it when it will be a memory, and normality will seem an unexpected and beautiful thing. We will love everything that has so far seemed futile to us. Every second will be precious. Swims in the sea, the sun until late, sunset, laughter. We will go back to laughing together. Strength and courage. See you soon!'

Sometimes there is nothing that can be done. When it rains, we wait for the sunshine. Loving God, your desire is for wholeness and wellbeing. We hold in tenderness and prayer the collective suffering of our world at this time. We grieve for precious lives lost and the vulnerable lives threatened. We ache for ourselves and our neighbours, standing before an uncertain future. Inspire our leaders to discern and choose wisely aligned with the common good. Help us to practice social- distancing and reveal to us new and creative ways to come together in spirit and in solidarity.

Hold us to a profound trust in your faithful presence, you, the God who does not abandon anyone.

The other interesting factor in all of this is that, as a people, we are not allowed to attend Mass. Mass has been streamed online and people are engaging in a new spiritual enterprise that may have long-term consequences regarding church attendance. Why not be spiritually engaged in a Mass streamed in the comfort of your living room rather than attending the same ceremony in a cold and unfriendly church?

I love the idea that a priest had in Italy. Even though his parishioners were not allowed to attend the Sunday Mass, he put photos of his people on the pews. What a Parish that must be!

Our bishops encouraged us to make a spiritual communion and many of the younger generation Catholics are mystified at the idea. These are the ones asking about 'a spiritual offertory collection'.

Zooming with Jesus and with each other.

For the last 23 Sundays, a group of us have met for a Liturgy of the Word. It was clear from the first meeting that a community of Catholics was being formed in prayer, in fellowship and in love. The foundations of this community were chiefly based in the Parish of Havant and Emsworth where most of the members lived. For most meetings, there were over 25 households on *Zoom,* with sometimes over 40 participants. Members ranged mostly in the over 50's age-group, but we had young people as well, including children, taking a full part in the liturgies. We had people from Basingstoke to Goring-by-Sea in West Sussex and even a granddaughter from Birmingham!

The format of the liturgy followed the Liturgy of the Word as in the Mass, but without the Eucharist. We had the Readings of the day, we sang hymns, we had a young mother, called Eleanor, sing the Psalm professionally most Sundays, we had prayers of the faithful. Fr. John Humphries and I alternated with a reflection on the Gospel of the day.

The liturgy lasted about forty minutes, but the session was opened 20 minutes before 9.00 a.m. At first, I did not appreciate the profound significance of the gathering time. People joined at different times, which gave those who had already joined to personally greet the newcomers. We could also call them by name since their names were on the screen.

Everyone knows how important it is to meet friends in the flesh, but the next best thing is to meet them virtually. In fact, sometimes we have a greater encounter at a distance. For me personally, the meeting was powerfully important, especially during the deepest lockdown.

This virtual liturgy was possible with the technical

expertise of Peter Agius who used his talents as a member of the lay Benedictine Community at Worth Abbey.
http://www.laybenedictines.org/bede

Here is what Richard Belfrage wrote to Peter a few days ago,

You deserve a medal for all the hard work you have put into organising the weekly liturgy for our parish community these last 5 months. The services have been truly inspirational, especially with so many taking an active part each week. All the singing, and especially Eleanor's singing of the Psalms, has always been beautiful. Frs Tom and John brought so much to the services with their eulogies and prayers. We were privileged and fortunate to have them.

Above all, you have kept us focused on the love of God and of our fellow parishioners during these stressful and difficult months. I can honestly say that for me, it has been my 'essential Sunday lockdown service', which has bought me so much joy, praying with my fellow parishioners.

Thank you so, so much Peter and all involved.

God Bless and Kind Regards,

Richard

The other significant development which I saw was how the participants grew in leadership roles.

There were several spin-offs that could be termed surprising until you considered the outstanding talents of those taking part.

People who were bereaved recently and others who were not well were called on or contacted electronically on a regular basis. They were also included in the Bidding Prayers. Personally, I was really beginning to enjoy incarceration when I had a delivery of lovely Lebanese cakes from a Sunday Morning 'Zoomer'.

There were extra blessings too, as some people did a virtual Pilgrimage to Canterbury. On 30 April, 35 of us set out for a special virtual journey to mark the 850th anniversary of the martyrdom of Thomas-à-Becket. The organisers and guides were Maureen and Stuart Thompson. All the Churches in Emsworth were invited to join in and there were enthusiastic messages from both Bishops of Portsmouth and a wonderful message of welcome from the Dean of Canterbury. There was a double importance for this venture in that both the Anglican Church in Warblington and the Catholic Church in Emsworth are dedicated to St. Thomas-à-Becket. By the time we arrived in Canterbury on Pentecost Sunday, we had over 100 pilgrims.

We also took part in 'Thy Kingdom Come' initiative where 60 people of all the local denominations took part. We joined the national service on Pentecost with messages from Pope Francis and the Archbishop of Canterbury.

www.emsworthchristians.com/events.html

The other revealing gift came from Jacky Chong who gave us two Novenas. Her first was a Novena, based on the Our Father, and her second Novena to Our Lady has just been published. See both attached or check out the second on *YouTube*

https://youtu.be/zNYV0niVXGA

A week resting with Covid-19

Because of lockdown I opted to revisit four of my favourite spiritual writers, John O' Donohue, Daniel O'Leary, Joyce Rupp and Anna Burke. In the process I was happy to balance the genders in equal measure. It goes without saying that, in difficult times, it is worth looking again at people who inspire us and enrich our lives. I really love these four spiritual heroes.

I decided to map out my week with some of the wonderful things they have shared with us for many years. I opted for the week because every day is a path of wonder with different invitations. Even in lockdown, no two days are the same, so I decided not to dodder but acknowledge that every moment of every day is a gift. Because something happened, we had not planned, everyone is more alert to the frailty and the wonder of life. In the following pages I am using John, Daniel, Joyce, and Anna as four loudspeakers for Covid-19. I refrain from quoting them directly because I wanted to personalise what they have written to make it my own for the times we are in.

I really set out, in this little endeavour, so that these great people would inspire me, enrich my spiritual journey even for seven days. But I was also aware that if they could do it for seven days, they could easily do the same for 365 days and every year.

In better ways than I had anticipated they reignited a prayerful liturgy and a spirituality in me. Most of this is new and exciting so I am delighted to share this reflection with you as reader. I hope that you will gain as much strength and inspiration as I have done.

One Week in Spiritual Lockdown
Monday~~~Nature

Monday became my nature day. I am blessed with a lovely garden and this year, my garden became a sanctuary and a haven of peace. Every morning, there is a special liturgy that says 'goodbye' to the darkness of the night and welcomes the light of a new day and a new week. In this liturgy, we find new beginnings breaking into colour with invitations to profound possibilities.

Because of lockdown I missed the opportunity to buy flower seeds in Spring, but I had saved Nasturtium seeds which I planted all over the garden. They flourished with lovely hearts that exuded love. This flower lets you know in a cheeky way that it loves you every moment. It is also a missionary disciple as it spreads out in all directions. Here is genius that causes wonder and surprise throughout the landscape.

This growth generates awe in most people, as well as in mountains, rivers and seas every year. We hardly notice the wonder it adds to the personality of nature. A life that reaches out is the only life worth living, as the life that does not take a risk is an unlived life.

Lockdown is a great opportunity for us to reach out in ways and directions we never imagined. That is one of the awe-inspiring things of Covid-19, in that millions of people reached out to neighbours and nations in need and sometimes, like the flower, risking everything, even risking death itself. Such is the sacrificial nature of all living things. Parish welfare personnel came into their own and, since March, I have had several phone calls from members of the St. Vincent de Paul Society.

I set up a prayer-line, only to be surprised that nearly everybody who requested prayer did so via email. This gave me the opportunity to send them copies of prayers I had sourced from my four heroes, with the invitation that we join together in praying the prayers three times a day for the specific intention. One man encouraged over 100 family and friends to join us in prayer each day. His wife has recovered fully and is now back home.

Monday is a day with nature in mind, especially the seeds of the Nasturtium, in which we miraculously find the seeds of hope, happiness, joy and especially compassion, a seed mentioned several times by my four gurus.

I am delighted to say that I come from a farming background in Co. Mayo and it is amazing that those origins have never left me. In fact, they are in my DNA. My origins breathe my vitality and everyone has the responsibility to ensure that breath is robust and healthy. Monday is a good day to breathe deeply of Mother Earth.

Tuesday~~~You as a Gift

Tuesday is a day to appreciate how precious we are. We are made in the image and likeness of God. We are embraced with love, believer or not, sinner or not, baptised, or not. God is hopelessly in love with us.

The caricature of an angry Father is heavily ingrained in the Catholic psychic. Some people have called this 'spiritual abuse'. The clouds of threats about hell, limbo and purgatory have savagely closed our minds and hearts to the all-embracing love of God. Lockdown is a great opportunity to bid farewell to such rubbish.

On Tuesday also you can hear the birds sing the praises of God.

Jesus invites us to think about the value of the sparrow and all birds in the sky. I think their singing is better this year than ever and, in the garden, I often try to imitate them with poor consequences. The effort itself is a prayer, especially now that we will not be able to sing in church. Even attempting to sing with nature we are soaring into the heights.

We are invited to seek information from the birds in the sky. Birds are highly qualified musicians and singers and it is a real therapy to pay attention to their ability to produce a perfect chorus with sublime orchestration.

All birds, even the greedy seagulls, invite us to become one with the angels. They take us in a new direction in which life is no longer safe or domesticated, while they remain our joyful guardians.

Tuesday is a great day of trust and care with divine providence for the smallest parts of our universe. Everything on earth is kissed by the love of God. Regardless of gender, race, colour, creed, or indeed behaviour. Everyone has the light of divinity. This really struck home with the *Black Lives Matter* movement which blasted into the mayhem of the pandemic.

As a Church, we have major issues here. In this respect, I was heartened by Hugh MacMahon's 'Finding the Way Back' in the June's issue of *The Furrow*. He at least is one missionary disciple prepared to admit the mistakes.

Tuesday can easily become every day for the rest of eternity.

Wednesday~~~*Black Lives Matter-* **All lives matter.**

Wednesday is very pro Covid-19. In the Church we have clericalism.   In life generally, we have individualism. Both have the same origins with the same appalling consequences - 'ME. ME syndrome'. False isolationism is the sin of the church and priests have lived it for decades. Self-isolate for long enough and you create a mystique and some people survive on the mystery for their whole lives. It is a pathetic myth.

All our core values, everything we do must be in the context that we are all citizens of the world. Our authentic identity is that we are residents of the universe. The wonderful saying, 'we are in this together' of Covid-19 must become the mantra of future generations. The dream for the future is destroyed by 'compulsive consumerism and collective selfishness' (Pope Francis).

If we address collective selfishness and remedy it, everyone is blessed with inestimable gifts. For one thing, our friends become incredibly special to us and we to them. There is a special if unusual beauty in having real friends who care for us, who pray for us each day.

There are many lonely frontiers we could never endure or cross without the love and care of true friends, in which I include family. We can be haunted and even destroyed by the ghosts of negativity, so it is not a luxury to have such friends but a necessity.

Many great spiritual people live out their faith on

Wednesday rather than on Sunday. Others do so because of Sunday. They have a storehouse of power and strength which they generously share in the public places where acute care is needed in our time.

50 years ago, the Second Vatican Council asked us to 'fix a steady gaze' on the marginalised of our time. Wednesday is a day to look at our fellow human beings from a different perspective in which the hostile becomes hospitable, the stranger can cast off the strangeness and everyone becomes our fellow human being. With *Black Lives Matter* we have a mountain to climb.

With that profound challenge we acknowledge the richness and beauty of other cultures and races. One of my great joys is travel and I have experienced the beauty of those races and cultures.

While we live in challenging and bleak days, what sustains me is beauty. Beauty is everywhere even in a bus with a sign 'Bus Full' but only eight people in it poles apart. I really enjoy all the TV programmes about rail travel. They let us in to a different world in which expert engineers added to the powerful beauty of nature. Around every engineering feat and every corner is profound beauty that invades the nostrils, the eyes, and the ears. Colour in its natural habitat bursts forth to encourage us each moment of life.

This is a beautiful day - make sure you register the word as it will make you beautiful.

Thursday~~~Death~~~Grief.

Many years ago, I provided pastoral care following the sudden death of a husband who was possessive of his wife. While arranging his funeral I casually said to the widow: 'Enjoy your freedom'. Many years later, she thanked me for those words although at the time she thought it was a strange statement. Old age brings a great freedom. As the body diminishes, the soul gets richer. Now I must admit when I read those words, I went into further lockdown with almost complete isolation for two days to ponder my soul getting richer at 75! Up to now, I thought the reverse was the case. But with my four luminaries, I have changed direction. The soul is engaged even in our sleep. There are rivers of dream thoughts all the time, every 24 hours for 365 days.

Old age is harvest time to ruminate on all that has happened in our lives. A wise woman in a shop in Moycullen said: "You never see a trailer following a hearse'. We take nothing with us and yet we take real treasures of interior things. Nursing homes have suffered remarkable numbers of deaths as a result of Covid-19 and I pondered on the pain, grief and sadness of the deaths of remarkable people. These people knew the chaff from the grain; they had harvested the goodness of life.

One of the great things is that we can keep them in memory. I vividly remember my mother, even though she died 45 years ago. For the important people in our lives, nothing is ever lost or forgotten. Memory is a sacramental liturgy and no wonder Jesus invited us to 'do this in memory of me'.

There is no education programme for getting old. You just get old. Some people allow the gravity of age to pull them down, while others look at the possibilities in which amazing things happen. I listened to a woman of 105 on the BBC Radio recently. She was asked what she looked forward to most, to which she replied: 'Going to the West End to see the latest musical'. How we view the future shapes the present and all our expectations create the future

Friday~~~Fasting.

Many years ago, seven of us undertook part of the Camino. All the recommendations of those who had been on the journey before us said we should travel lightly. Two days into the journey some of us cast off some of the rubbish we thought was necessary.

Travelling lightly is a great lesson in discovering what is important and essential for life. But it also liberates us to really engage with others, or indeed, to engage with your inner self.

Everyone collects things in the journey of life - some are essential, and some are just rubbish. The bottom line is that we are entrusted with hidden treasures. Sometimes we need to sell the field to find the pearl of great price.

Lockdown has presented me with daily reminders to let go. I enjoy what I have but I do not necessarily hold on to it, and the more I let go, the happier I am. I am approaching retirement, and this is a great preparation to discover what is important and what I can let flow down the river of life. Life is much better when we declutter not only the material rubbish but the spiritual rubbish too. What a hoard of spiritual rubbish have I collected in my 47 years as a priest?

Fasting is part of the de-cluttering. For a week, I monitored the adverts on TV and 90% of them were about food. Yet there is a huge growth in the need for foodbanks throughout the land. In the Gospel, the disciples wanted to send the people away so that they could buy food for themselves in the surrounding towns and villages. Jesus says this is not an option: 'Give them something to eat'.

These are words of a social revolution.

All are called to the banquet and all have a right to the food on the table. To make sure the table has food is real fasting. To say we have only five barley loaves and two fish is to miss the point. Jesus does not decry the meagre offerings, but he releases them in ways beyond belief. Daily, Jesus challenges our resources and when the Lord invited the disciples to distribute the food, the dream of communion and compassion became a reality.

Since March 2020 we have millions of people 'eat as much as they wanted', due to the fasting of others. That is a real miracle of communion and this is an integral part of being a flower of Jesus.

Saturday~~~Mercy Day.

Have you ever noticed that all the people Jesus called were flawed? He accepted them with love because he wanted to lead them to wholeness. While those, scribes and pharisees, who thought they were perfect, he reprimanded severely.

God even comes into our failures and we need to move to a place where we accept our weaknesses. Then we can accept the cup of mercy. In lockdown we have had loads of opportunities to see the flaws and still let God in.

'The sins you forgive, there are forgiven, the sins you retain they are retained' (John 2:23). Jesus did not give that commission specifically to any set group of people, it is given to everyone. In the Church we have manipulators and controllers of the mercy of God. A few years ago, we had a Year of Mercy and that year is ongoing as the door of God's mercy is always open.

There is a strange irony in that we were able to have 'virtual communion' but no 'virtual forgiveness'. When our churches could be opened again some bishops announced that the churches were now open for Confessions, which perpetuate the Catholic guilt complex. Our churches are open for prayer, first and foremost.

As a faith community, we should be ashamed that there are people who have done wrong, but we cannot or perhaps more correctly will not forgive. I know good people who did stupid things 40-50 years and even though they still attend Mass, they have not been forgiven. Everyone in ministry should read Mt.18:22 at least once a week. Forgiveness is close companion of compassion and both are an integral part of the journey of life -never more so than during Covid-19. I have given Absolution over the phone to several people in the last 100 days. In one tragic case, I did so with great humility because the person was close to death and her priest could not risk administering the Sacrament of the Sick in person.

Sunday~~~Resurrection.

I have kept the best until the last or as the first!

Death is an unseen, unknown companion who walks with us every moment. We should take comfort from our travelling partner because life is full of little and large deaths.

We are invited daily to allow death to become a true companion, so that when the time comes, you can both walk together into the life promised by Jesus. 'I am the Resurrection and the Life' (John 11:25). In that life in abundance, there is no more darkness, no more pain, no more suffering, sadness or separation.

When two people left Jerusalem one morning, they assumed that Golgotha was the tragic result, that everything was a failure. They went west to forget the past or find a new meaning to their lives. But then, their eyes were opened as they sat at table. The one they did not know was blessing and breaking in a way that was instantly recognisable. The giving and the sharing were the icing on the cake. This was nothing more than was promised.

What could they do? Well, you have only one choice - to tell the others that Emmaus in not just a place but an encounter. Now that our churches are open once more, they are not just places, but encounters.

In March 2020, we too left Jerusalem behind with our heads cast low. We talked to each other through modern media and we talked to each other about what had happened. Our hearts were downcast.

This is not the end of the week but the beginning.

Now, we become the Artist who looks at the marble and sees the hidden angel.

The Farmer who looks at the winter fields and sees the rich harvest.

The Mystic who looks at the caterpillar and sees the butterfly.

The Midwife who looks at a distressed body and sees a beautiful new baby.

The Teacher who looks at the students and sees mighty potential.

The Prophet who sees the dawning light of every new day.

Jesus who looks at sinners and sees grace.

This is exactly where we started this journey in the light of Monday morning. Here we now have the array of the great Northern Light.

Books absorbed:-

John O'Donohue:-
Benedictus, Anam Cara, Eternal Echoes.

Bantam Press.

Walking on the Pastures of Wonder. Veritas

Joyce Rupp:-

The Cup of Our Life, Ave Maria Press.

Boundless Compassion. Sorin Books.

Constant Hope. Twenty Third Publications.

Walking in a Relaxed Manner. Orbis Books.

<u>Daniel O'Leary:</u> -

An Astonishing Secret. Columba Press.

<u>*Anna Burke:*</u> -

While they were at Table. Veritas.

A letter I had published in *The Tablet* 26th April 2020

Following on from the report in last week's *Tablet* that the congregation of Wrexham Diocese trebled at the virtual Easter Services this year, I have just had the privilege of taking part in a *Zoom* Community Liturgy for the Second Sunday of Easter. The Liturgy of the Word lasted 45 minutes. It was prayerful; there was good singing; it was thought-provoking, with a lovely interaction between the participants. There were 31 people involved. There was real long-distance fellowship, humour, and no collection. This new community is a lay initiative, and it will meet every Sunday at 9.00 a.m. This is merely one of numerous initiatives in which people are engaging because of Covid-19. I heard that Fr. Richard Gibbons, the Parish Priest of Knock, in three days over Easter blessed 900 homes with their occupants. The people of that parish will never forget such brave a gesture as they saw their priest blessing them from the front gate.

Beyond lockdown, we all need to reflect on the many different forms of worship which are emerging, because a spiritual powerhouse is opening up before us that we have never encountered before. A new Church could well be a staying at home community and not just for the elderly and infirm. We are encountering the beginning of a powerful and radical form of prayerful worship. I hope you enjoyed reading these echoes as much as I enjoyed writing them.

Writing them was like watching the first daffodils on a Spring day. It was as enriching as the rays of sunlight on a sunny day on the Solent. It was inspiring as standing on the top of Croagh Patrick to wonder at the beauty of Clew Bay. It was as comforting as sitting with family and friends in a pub west of the Shannon. It was as uplifting as meeting a school friend after 50 years of separation.

Blessings Galore!

"The best of a book is not the thought which it contains, but the thought which it suggests, just as the charm of music dwells not in the tones but in the echoes of our hearts"

John Greenleaf Whittier

Acknowledgements

Rt Rev Crispian Hollis, for the Foreword to this publication and for being Bishop of Portsmouth 1989-2012.

Grania Egan for editing professionally.

Jacky Chong for her insights, and recommendations.

Anne W. Purdie for Artwork on front and back covers.

Sarah Keen for compiling this book.

Bridie Stringer for her professional insights and observations.

Brendan Walsh, Editor of *The Tablet*, for positive encouragement.

Jay Kettle-Williams, Editor of the *Portsmouth People*.

To Editors of *The Furrow*, *Intercom* and *The Pastoral Review*.

Fr. Tom Lane, CM President of All Hallows College for leading 240 seminarians through the exciting years of post-Vatican II Church.

Fr. Kevin Condon CM for encouraging all rural seminaries to listen to the birds who sing the scriptures.

Fr. Clement Tiger SJ for the correct pronunciation of big words.

Diana Klein for her expert comments on all the articles published in *The Tablet*.

Fathers Tony Pennicott, Tom Taaffe, and Padraig Faughnan for sharing some of the spiritual expeditions in many foreign parts.

Fr. Roy Bennett, Chaplain to Reading Gaol.

John and Loli Kieran, Alison and Tim McCann, Deirdre and David Barrett, Maureen and Stuart

Thompson, Mary Huntley, Julia Corps, Minnie Greayer for their generous enrichment of my priesthood.

For all those who have joined me on pilgrimages over many years and especially John Kieran, flight expert extraordinary.

All the people whom I have known in those Parishes I have worked in.

Especially to my Family for love, support, and inspiration.

Printed in Great Britain
by Amazon

57432826R00135